FEAR, NO MORE

FEAR GOD EVERMORE

Sandy!
Praying that this
book connects
you to God in a
way that makes you
an even more dangerous
freedom fighter!
+Benjamin
Ps 19:9

BENJAMIN GILMORE

Fear, No More: Fear God Evermore

Copyright © 2019 by Truth Is Everything, LLC

Unless otherwise noted, Scripture taken from the New King James Version®. Copyright © 1982 by Thomas Nelson. Used by permission. All rights reserved.

Scripture quotations marked (NASB) are taken from the New American Standard Bible® (NASB), copyright © 1960, 1962, 1963, 1968, 1971, 1972, 1973, 1975, 1977, 1995 by The Lockman Foundation. Used by permission. www.Lockman.org.

Scripture quotations marked (NIV) are taken from the Holy Bible, New International Version®, NIV®. Copyright © 1973, 1978, 1984, 2011 by Biblica, Inc.™ Used by permission of Zondervan. All rights reserved worldwide. www.zondervan.com. The "NIV" and "New International Version" are trademarks registered in the United States Patent and Trademark Office by Biblica, Inc.™

Scripture quotations marked (NLT) are taken from the Holy Bible, New Living Translation, copyright ©1996, 2004, 2015 by Tyndale House Foundation. Used by permission of Tyndale House Publishers, Inc., Carol Stream, Illinois 60188. All rights reserved.

ISBN: 978-1-083027-39-9

Library of Congress Control Number: 2019910600

Printed in the United States of America

19 20 21 22 23 — 5 4 3 2 1

Published by

Bedford, Texas

TABLE OF CONTENTS

INTRODUCTION

MY WIFE, JENNIFER, and I were newlyweds when we went
on our first camping trip. Telling tales of nature and fires
and tents, I had really boosted the experience in my wife's
mind. However, a frighteningly dark night, a flooded tent, and
strange sounds were enough of an "experience" to make our
first camping trip our last one. (Maybe we will go again one
day, but I'm not pressing my luck.)

Our first camping trip makes a fun story for us to share, but
stories of brushes with fear aren't always something to smile
at. This is especially true when an experience with fear is less
like a brush and more like a diabolical tackle.

I think that it is safe to say that the real-life experiences
with fear we all have encountered are enough for us to want to
know how to beat it.

Here are my personal reasons for wanting to beat fear:

Jennifer and I had not been together long (four months
dating, two months "official") when life hit. Her heart began
racing out of control, pumping at over 250 beats per minute.
Jennifer's body shook as if by some unseen outside force.
I was in Houston for a wedding, and she was in Dallas. The
distance seemed to make the feelings of terror that much
worse. Unable to slow down her heart rate, she was rushed to
the ER.

Life seemed to hang by a thread at that moment. I feared the worst. Had I come to find the love of my life only to lose her? Had beauty found me only to fade away like a sunset on a day that I prayed would never end? Fear gripped me. Fear gripped her.

Fast forward a couple of years, and we found ourselves staring fear in the face again. I had been dealing with mono, and my tonsils were cutting off my airway. Medicines weren't working to shrink them, so the tonsils had to go. Surgery was set, and it went smoothly.

According to my doctor, this painful and not-fun procedure was supposed to involve a nine-day recovery. I took time off and ate pudding, Jell-O, and anything soft that my sensitive throat would allow. (I do *not* recommend tomato soup, by the way.) Each day had its challenges but nothing to fret about.

Then came day nine. I awoke around 7:00 AM with something in my throat. Getting up from my bed, I went to the sink to discover that the mystery liquid was blood. A blood vessel had ruptured, and I was bleeding out. I couldn't stop it. Life was leaving me like an old friend right before my eyes.

Grabbing a large cup, we headed to the ER. I stayed calm enough through the whole ordeal, but I'll never forget what it was like to watch life leave me. There was nothing like it.

How could this happen? My doctor told me there was only a three percent chance that something like this could happen, and I somehow landed in this percentile. I had done nothing wrong. I was merely a statistical anomaly.

Imagine the fear that gripped me two years later when my father's body was ravaged for far too long by an unknown illness. Finally, and potentially too late, he was diagnosed with Rocky Mountain Fever. Having gone so long without proper treatment, recovery was questionable. We were told that three percent of such cases end in death.

If three percent was enough to send me into emergency surgery while watching my life slip away, three percent seemed good enough to allow me to watch my father's life slip away too.

Fear was there. I felt it. I fought it. I prayed.

And again fear filled the room the night that doctors said a CT scan was necessary on my pregnant wife. Diagnosed with a possible blood clot in the chest, we were left alone in a room to decide: get the CT scan and risk giving our unborn daughter cancer, or skip the procedure and risk the blood clot killing both Jennifer and our baby. How could anyone make this choice?

Where was God in that moment of fear? We cried out to Him. We prayed.

These are some of the stories in my life that give me the reason to say, "Fear, no more!" I'm tired of nights where sleep is fleeting because fear is fighting. I'm tired of fear ravaging my soul and my family. It's one thing my wife and I would love NOT to pass down to our daughter as a part of our legacy. After all, fear is a legacy issue. The battles we fight today will impact the battles our children fight tomorrow.

———

Fear is a legacy issue.
The battles we fight today will impact the
battles our children fight tomorrow.

What is your story? Are you ready to overcome fear? To do so, we have to know exactly what we are fighting. Let's begin the road to victory by finding the definition of fear together. When we rightly understand *what* we fight, we can rightly know *how* to fight, and then we will win.

1

JOURNEY TOWARD FEAR

NOT SO LONG AGO, an eight-year-old boy awoke suddenly to flashes of lightning and the crackling sound of thunder. Light invaded his room, each evil flash followed by a loud BOOM! The boy nervously looked toward his open bedroom door. Somehow the dark hallway seemed to grow increasingly darker between each flash. *What kind of evil might be out there?* he wondered.

Now if you have ever been an eight-year-old boy (or girl), you probably know there are only three reasons to wake up in the middle of the night: storms, nightmares, and full bladders. For this boy, the storm was definitely a nightmare, and his bladder was announcing (quite forcefully) that it had reached maximum capacity. He faced a conundrum: to venture across his room, into the hall, and down to the bathroom promised untold horrors, yet to stay put was to embrace certain bedwetting. (He realized the latter would not be as easily forgiven as it might have been just three short years before.)

If the power would just come back on! If the storm would just go away! Then the boy realized there was a third option. Reaching out cautiously (after all, you never know what might be lurking under the bed), he grabbed his trashcan and ... well, I think you get the idea. He was able to relieve the pounding pressure in his bladder without the embarrassment of wetting the bed and without the terror of venturing down the hall.

Confession time: that eight-year-old boy was me. And while my childhood fear now makes for a funny anecdote, we all know that fear doesn't always offer such amusing tales. We've all lived stories so intense that we don't even like to think about them, let alone share them with others. I am certainly no exception.

As an adult, I began to look at the concept of fear both through my own experiences and through Scripture. I wondered, *What if fear is not what we thought it was? What if we aren't simply believing lies about our fears—what if we are believing lies about fear itself?*

─────

What if we aren't simply believing lies about our fears—what if we are believing lies about fear itself?

Fear. We've all run from it, fought it, and at times, been overcome by it. As if buried alive under a heaping mound of dirt, we gasp for air, digging with all our emotional and spiritual might. If we manage to claw our way out, we then struggle to clean fear's stain from our battered souls. We limp forward, afraid to fall under fear's control once again. We fight and fight and fight, always with fear's nagging voice in the background. Even when we do have a victory, it taunts, "So what? You'll never get rid of me."

No one is immune to fear. I've tried talking my way out of it, puffing up my chest to intimidate it, and even avoiding its sources in my life. However, none of these methods have worked.

Perhaps you are like me. Maybe you have wrestled with fear and lost more times that you care to admit. Worn down and undone by the struggle, you have surrendered to a life directed and consumed by fear.

If you struggle with fear, you aren't alone. Fear is the disease that infects every person, regardless of age, gender, race, intelligence, or socioeconomic status. Here are just a few of our society's top fears:

- corrupt government officials
- terrorist attacks
- lack money for the future
- government restrictions
- death of a loved one
- economic or financial collapse
- identity theft
- people we love becoming seriously ill[1]

These fears don't happen by accident. They have a source. We live in a world that breeds fear and then capitalizes upon it. We look to the news for facts, but we find fear instead. After all, television networks care only about one thing: ratings. Ratings go up when viewers are kept on the edge of their seats, and what better hook is there than fear?

Fear doesn't just seize adults; it captures our children too. My daughter is only three years old, so the nightly news might hold her attention for just a second. Cartoons, on the other hand, are much more engaging (for me too, I'll admit). Just

1. Mary Bowerman, "Survey Reveals What Americans Fear the Most," USA Today, October 12, 2016, accessed November 03, 2018, https://www.usatoday.com/story/news/nation-now/2016/10/12/survey-top-10-things-americans-fear-most/91934874/.

like any adult sitcom or soap opera, these "innocent" shows often have a plot that involves fear as the problem in need of a solution. The issue is that my daughter doesn't just recognize the solution; she catches the problem as well. She may not be able to define fear, but phrases such as "That's scary!" or "I'm scared!" are now part of her vocabulary.

If you are a believer in Jesus Christ, you have an enemy who will try to use fear to rob you of God's destiny for your life. Jesus tells us in John 10:10, "The thief does not come except to steal, and to kill, and destroy." The verse doesn't end with this discouraging news, though. Instead, Jesus continues, "I have come that they may have life, and that they may have *it* more abundantly."

Join me through the pages of this book as we embark on a journey toward fear. "Toward fear?" you may ask with disbelief. Yes, indeed. Many people say we must face our fears, but I say we must face fear itself. With God leading us, we will journey toward our foe and stare it down. We'll find what lurks beneath it and overcome it with nothing short of brutal intentionality.

Writing this book has been quite a journey. In February 2016, I felt God leading me to study fear. Fueled by His Word and a deep desire to help my wife and myself find freedom, I began. Several months later, I had an opportunity to teach a class at my church. This class opened my eyes to how widespread the fear epidemic really is. A year later, I felt the Lord ask me to take another, even bolder step: write this book.

I believe every person wants to be free, and the journey to freedom has important landmarks called hearing, faith, obedience, and worship. Hearing is the first link in a powerful chain-breaking process. Without hearing, we cannot have the faith needed to move forward, and without faith, we likely won't be obedient to what God says. We must hear, have faith, and obey if we are going to overcome fear. Only then can we worship God and live truly free lives.

As you turn the pages of this book, please don't merely read my words. Invite God to speak to you through each line and every chapter. Allow Him to speak directly to your heart. I've heard it said many times that "the words of men inspire, but the Word of God transforms." I am humbled and grateful for the chance to inspire, but I pray even more that you experience true transformation as you hear the voice of God.

———

> We must hear, have faith, and obey if we are going to overcome fear. Only then can we worship God and live truly free lives.

Fear doesn't make sense from the outside, so we must examine it from the inside. In this book, you will not find an exhaustive list of verses to combat each and every fear known to mankind. My goal is not to teach you how to combat specific fears with Scripture, though I could certainly recommend several good books that do just that.[2] My desire is to get behind fear and answer these questions: *Where does fear come from? What purpose does it serve?* Once we find fear's root, we can rip it out of the ground and expose it. It's time to realize our authority. It's time to take back fear.

---

2. Neil Anderson and Rich Miller, *Freedom from Fear.*
John Bevere, *The Fear of the Lord. Breaking Intimidation.*
Max Lucado, *Fearless.*
Jentezen Franklin, *Fear Fighters.*

God, please help us see Your truth. Open our minds and hearts to receive whatever the Holy Spirit has to say. Give us eyes to see. Give us ears to hear. We want Your freedom to reign in our lives. In Jesus' name, Amen.

2

HEARING IS EVERYTHING

Now the Lord had said to Abram:
"Get out of your country,
From your family
And from your father's house,
To a land that I will show you.
I will make you a great nation;
I will bless you
And make your name great;
And you shall be a blessing.
I will bless those who bless you,
And I will curse him who curses you;
And in you all the families of the earth shall be blessed."

—Genesis 12:1–3

I HAVE A SERIOUS issue with allowing my mind to sit in the future more than it needs to. I try to tell it to come back to the present, but I'm not always successful. It was in the midst of one of these times that my mind began to think on the prospect of turning thirty-three. I was in my mid-twenties, and suddenly thirty-three didn't seem so far away.

Thirty-three might seem like a strange number for my mind to land on, but Jesus was thirty-three when He died on the cross. That thought led to this thought: *I'm going to die when I turn thirty-three.*

This may seem like an extreme statement, but earlier in my life, I pointed the top desire of my heart toward living as Jesus lived. I wanted to love as He loved and be like Him in every way possible. In that moment of thinking to the future, in came this powerful thought: *at thirty-three, I am going to die as Jesus died.*

Until I was 32, I could sometimes push the thought away. However, once I turned 32, the thought emerged as a constant fear. Dying at 33 seemed like a destined reality. This fear was killing my peace by speaking death over my future. I heard the message loud and clear.

The key to my journey toward fear started right there: *I heard.* Hearing is the first step on the path to fear, and thus it is also the first step that we must take together in this book. We must understand the importance of hearing in order to understand the role it plays in the way fear dominates our lives.

Hearing is something that we do each and every day. Sometimes we hear with our ears, but much more often, we hear with our hearts and our eyes. We read the body language of the store clerk as we walk up to the counter to make a purchase. Before a word is said, we know their mood, and whether this will be a pleasant experience or not. As soon as we see the scowl plastered on their face, we hear loud and clear, "This is *not* going to be a good experience."

Growing up I heard (and understood) body language *very* well. I wasn't very good at communicating with attractive girls, but I sure could read their body language! I would walk up to a girl, and though she didn't say a word, her body language told me, "Um, no thanks!" loud and clear. (I would then keep walking or pretend that something else gained my attention.)

Hugging is another example of unspoken language. When we embrace a special someone, it's as if their heart sings a song to ours! It's beautiful. In a warm embrace, messages of acceptance and love pass back and forth—heart to heart.

In the 1970s, Doctor Albert Mehrabian studied the effects of non-verbal communication, specifically when in conflict with verbal communication.[3] Imagine if someone came into the room that I'm writing in right now and told me, "Nice beard." Their shoulders are square to me, there's a twinkle in their eye, and a broad smile crosses their face. How would I feel? Probably warm and fuzzy. I'd look at them and say, "Why thank you! I grew it myself, by God's grace!" (No, seriously, by God's grace. When I was nine years old, I realized my father couldn't grow a beard, so I prayed and asked God for facial hair. Prayer answered!)

Now imagine if someone came into the room and said those exact same words, but instead of a pleasant expression, they had a smirk and furrowed eyebrows. How would I feel then? I'd likely feel insulted and offended. When non-verbal communication competes with verbal communication, the non-verbal cues speak louder every time.

Dr. Mehrabian developed the 7–38–55 Communication Model. This model states that 55% of communication is visual, 38% is non-verbal, and only 7% is verbal! This tells us that we are receiving messages *constantly*—we are *always* hearing, even when those around us aren't using words. If we

---

3. Patty Mulder, "Communication Model by Albert Mehrabian," Tools Hero, September 12, 2018, accessed February 13, 2019, https://www.toolshero.com/communication-skills/communication-model-mehrabian/.

only pay attention to the messages that come to us by words, we will miss much of what is being communicated to us. What we miss may just be to our demise.

The messages we hear affect the way we see the world. It's one reason why God tells us to keep good company around us (1 Corinthians 15:33; Psalm 1:1), that life and death are in the power of the tongue (Proverbs 18:21), and that we should be careful how we hear (Luke 8:18). Lethal darts are firing toward us constantly.

———

The messages we hear affect the way we see the world.

When we hear the wrong things, they affect the way we interact with the world around us. For example, if those we spend time with tell us that everyone constantly lies, then we will walk through this life mistrusting all that people say to us. It will cause us to hold people at a distance and rob us of the opportunity for real relationships. You cannot get close to people you don't trust, and you cannot trust those whom you believe are lying. Even more dangerously, it might give us a false sense of permission to be liars ourselves.

Hearing is a big deal—bigger than we think. Hearing is everything. It's true for you, it's true for me, and it was true for Abraham as well. Imagine this:

Your brother dies. Your father, perhaps looking for a change to help erase the hurt of his loss or maybe feeling a nudge on the inside to move, takes you, your wife, and your nephew on a long journey to a place you have never been. Your only other living brother decides to stay behind with his wife and family, probably never to be seen again. Saying goodbye to two brothers in one lifetime is a whole lot to process emotionally, but you are committed to following your father and to being a loyal son.

The long journey is exhausting and relentless. Stopping in a city sharing a name much like your deceased brother's, your father ends his trip. You never quite know the inner convictions of your father. You never find out if his journey ended prematurely out of old age or out of a broken heart, but there he decided to stay.

Content to stay with your father, you begin imagining what life in this city will be like for you and your wife. You begin to settle down. This place seems far enough to go from the sadness that you and your father share.

Then you hear God.

In Genesis 12, God speaks to Abram. God *speaks*. Abram *hears*. Sometimes it's hard to know if you have heard God. It can be scary and uncertain, especially when the voice you hear tells you to do something as risky as leaving everything behind. "God, is that You?" we ask. The prospect of following through with what you hear can feel quite scary for many reasons.

God told Abram to leave his country (the place he felt safe), his father (the one who made him feel safe), and his relatives (the people with whom he could safely do life). To Abram, it must have felt like God asked Him to leave everything! I wonder if Abram thought, *What if this voice isn't God's but my own? What if my family thinks I'm crazy? What if I can't find food? What if ...*

It's easy to look with amazement at the promise in Genesis 12:1–3. Who wouldn't want to become a great nation, have a great name, and have God's blessing cover your future generations? However, we often overlook the part where Abram had to leave everything behind to receive that promise.

Abram had to obey before he could receive, and obedience was as simple as doing what he heard God say. It's not always easy to feel confident that you have heard God, especially when He makes what seems to be such a tall order. It would have been easier to say, "Get thee behind me, Satan. Quit telling me to leave my hurting family!"

For Abram, and for us, hearing is vital. Without hearing, the promise goes unreceived. Without hearing, we'd probably never move away from the comfortable known into the scary unknown. We likely stay stuck somewhere between the place of loss and death and the place of life and promise.

What does this have to do with fear? Everything! The journey to fear—and freedom—begins with hearing. *Hearing. Is. Everything.*

———

The journey to fear—and freedom—begins with hearing.

3

WHY HEARING IS EVERYTHING

So then faith *comes* by hearing, and hearing by the word of God.

—Romans 10:17

Reason One: Your fight depends on it.

Where did the thought that I was going to die at the age of 33 come from? Was it a fabrication of my own mind? Was it God's divine warning to my heart letting me know what was to come? (After all, John 16:13 says the Holy Spirit tells us of things to come). Or was it a diabolical, subliminal message implanted in my brain by some sort of conspiracy? Maybe.

Whose voice are you listening to? Who is interpreting all of the happenings around you? John 8:44 tells us this about Satan:

> "He was a murderer from the beginning, and does not stand in the truth, because there is no truth in him. When he speaks a lie, he speaks from his own resources, for he is a liar and the father of it."

Have you noticed that the more you hear a liar tell a story, the more elaborate and lengthier it gets? Even after you have figured out that the person is fabricating their story, they keep going! It's as if they're hoping to win you over eventually with a really convincing plot twist!

Our enemy is no exception. As the father of lies, Satan talks and talks and ... well, you get the idea. He never stops! So long as you will give him your ear, he will fill it.

Like most kids, I was a terrible liar. My parents could see right through my tall tales. When I grew older, though, I got really good at it. Want to know my secret? If you asked me a question, I would only answer with enough information to satisfy your curiosity but not offer the complete picture. I would purposefully give only the details and facts of the story that would allow you to draw the conclusion that I wanted you to draw—a conclusion that was nowhere near the truth. I was devious. I was deceptive. I was a liar.

Satan, the father of lies, loves to give us *just* enough facts to cause us to draw the conclusion that he wants us to draw, and it's *always* an incomplete picture. How do I know? Because lies never provide the whole picture. The whole picture is the truth. Because we can't argue the facts that the enemy provides us (they are facts, after all), we buy into his version of reality—his version of truth.

———

Satan, the father of lies, loves to give us *just* enough facts to cause us to draw the conclusion that he wants us to draw, and it's *always* an incomplete picture.

For example, let's say that while driving down the road, you hit a nail. Your tire goes flat, and now you have an unexpected expense. Immediately, frustration hits you, and the following facts run through your mind:

- My tire is flat, and I will probably have to buy another one.
- A new tire is not inexpensive.
- I have a lot of other expenses this month.
- I don't know how all of these expenses will be covered.

Who do you think is reminding you of all these facts? Let me answer that for you. It's the same one who draws conclusions from these facts for you and offers them as truths that sound a lot like this: *You're not going to make it. You have no hope. You're ruined. You are a failure.* If you haven't already guessed it, that's the voice of the enemy.

In life, if we are listening to a voice other than God's, that voice will lead us in a destructive direction. It may sound like a coach, a parent, a teacher, or a friend from the "good ol' days." These voices ring like old bells in our minds. When we mess up, one of them is quick to jump in and assess us, the situation, and God for us. However, if any voice doesn't agree with God's Word and what it says about His nature and character, then you are being led off a cliff! And for many people, the name of that cliff is fear. It can be a fear of death, rejection, loneliness, failure, not having enough, or anything else.

So what is truth? We must learn how to recognize what it is as well as what it isn't. While a lie from the enemy is a conclusion drawn from a limited number of facts, truth is the conclusion drawn from *all* facts inside and outside of the universe, past, present, and future. *But how can anyone know all that?* you may ask. I'll admit I don't even know *half* the facts in front of me, much less those past, present, future, etc.

While a lie from the enemy is a conclusion drawn from a limited number of facts, truth is the conclusion drawn from all facts inside and outside of the universe, past, present, and future.

Honestly, only One can see all of those facts. Only One holds the truth. That person's name is God, and He wants to speak to you about your situation. He wants to speak to you about your fear.

The simple answer to overcoming fear and walking right with God would appear to be "Just listen to God's voice, not the voice of the enemy." To that I would say enthusiastically, "Absolutely!" But how many of us know that concept yet still live lives influenced by, riddled with, or consumed by fear? I know I have. I know my wife has. And I know we have had enough of it and don't want our children to live with that same burden.

So how do we hear God's voice and make sure that it is the primary voice we are using to discover what the truth is? In his book *Frequency,* Pastor Robert Morris describes 10 ways God speaks to us:

1. Circumstances
2. Wise Counsel
3. Peace
4. People
5. Dreams and Visions
6. Our Thoughts
7. Natural Manifestations
8. Supernatural Manifestations

9. The Bible

10. A Whisper[4]

Maybe the idea of hearing God's voice is new to you. Or perhaps you have been hearing God's voice for years. Either way, I encourage you to *practice*. Why? Because the voice you listen to will determine the outcome of your fight. Remember: *hearing is everything.*

Once you hear, you then must choose whose voice to agree with. The voice you agree with is the voice that you empower to shape your life (Matthew 6:10).

———

The voice you agree with is the voice that
you empower to shape your life.

Reason Two: Your friendship depends on it.

I once played in a soccer match that had a few unfortunate turns of events. They weren't unfortunate for me, but they were for another young man. This guy showed up to the game for the same reason as me: to play soccer and hopefully win. His day ended differently than mine on several levels.

As the match progressed, I attempted to clear the ball out of our half of the field with a massive kick. The ball didn't make it far, though. The young man on the other team blocked my kick—with his face! He was in such pain that the referee stopped the game for a moment. Then my injured opponent stood on the sideline, drinking water and waiting for the pain to subside.

---

4. Robert Morris, *Frequency* (Nashville: W Publishing Group, 2016), 122–124.

Once again I saw the ball coming my way. I kicked it as hard as I could, but my foot didn't connect with the ball the way I had hoped. The ball careened off the field and went toward my already-injured opponent.

As if in slow motion, I watched the ball head straight for the bottom of his water bottle.

This normally would not have been a big deal, but his water bottle was connected to a very thick plastic straw that happened to be in his mouth at that very moment. As the ball made contact, blood spewed from his mouth, and tears gushed from his eyes. My opponent's game was over well before the final whistle blew.

After the game, my opponent approached me to finish a fight that I was unaware existed. Apparently, my accidental contacts were a bit too coincidental to him to be seen as anything other than an assault. He was ready to fight.

At that moment, I froze. *My first fight. What does one do? Do I fight? I love Jesus. Do Jesus-lovers fight? Is this the part where I turn the other cheek? Do I …*

As I searched for the correct response, my teammate stepped in front of me. "You'll have to come through me first," he retorted to whatever challenge my opponent placed before me. Then another of my teammates stepped between myself and my would-be attacker. "You'll have to come through me too." His words were music to my ears!

As each and every one of my teammates stepped in front of me, I found myself at the back of a very large team, and my opponent found himself turning and walking away. It was incredible! What a difference the right friends in the right place make!

As great as those friends were at that moment, I have always been a little jealous of Moses and his relationship with his Friend. Exodus 33:11 says, "The Lord spoke to Moses face to face, as a man speaks to his friend." *Face to face.* Amazing! Can you imagine what that was like?

There is nothing like meeting face to face with friends to catch up, learn more about each other, and connect. In a world of social media, face to face conversations are a lost art to many. It is the cry of my heart that I would be able to meet with God in this way.

It gets even better, though. Psalm 103:7 tells us,

He made known His ways to Moses,
His acts to the sons of Israel.

God not only spoke to Moses *as a friend*, but He also told Moses things that friends share with each other! While God was telling His people about His acts, He was giving Moses a look behind the scenes at His ways. Talk about amazing! Wouldn't it be great to have that sort of relationship with God?

Moses wasn't the first person to have this relationship with God (Adam and Eve were), and it's God's intention that Moses not be the last. James 2:23 tells us, "'Abraham believed God, and it was accounted to him for righteousness.' And he was called the friend of God." Abraham was called *the friend of God*. How is such a relationship possible? I want it! Don't you?

It's simple, really. It comes by hearing.

Have you ever tried to have a friendship with someone who would not hear you? You talked and talked, but they ignored you, or even worse, they talked over you? It's terribly annoying. A one-way conversation is the perfect formula for a stagnant (or dying) relationship.

I was raised in a church environment that greatly empha-
sized the importance of relationship with God (and rightfully
so). In the mix of things, the mantra "relationship, not
religion" was birthed in my heart. As I progressed on my
journey of faith, though, I began to see something in my life
and in the lives of those around me that Dr. Jim Richards so
eloquently describes in *The Gospel of Peace*.[5] He says that
many people talk about relationship, but they are really
talking about relationship with religion, not with God.

It's easy to get caught up in relationship with religion.
When we live life as a one-way conversation with God, we
begin to define what pleases Him (His reactions to our
displays of affection) by our ability to meet the expectations
set by our religion (man's attempt to get to God). When we
check enough of the boxes, we feel as if we are pleasing Him,
and when we don't, we seek reconciliation. In doing so, we
become another sad story of empty religion—striving and
working but never achieving.

———

> When we live life as a one-way conversation with God,
> we begin to define what pleases Him (His reactions to our
> displays of affection) by our ability to meet the expectations
> set by our religion (man's attempt to get to God).

When we see someone talking to a lifeless, man-made,
inanimate object, we call that person crazy. We want to tell
them, "There is no life there; that object can't talk back."

---

5. Richards, Jim B. *The Gospel of Peace*. Huntsville: Impact Ministries,
   1995. 135.

Religion is no different. It is a lifeless institution erected like buildings of old to reach the heavens. If you ever see me talking to a building, please kindly interrupt me.

Want to have a real relationship with God? Want to be His friend? Jesus said only what He heard His Father say (John 12:49), and He did only what He saw His Father do (John 5:19). That is how we are to live in relationship with God. It's how Moses lived. It's how Abraham lived. We must hear for every step, every day.

John 16:13 gives us Jesus' powerful promise:

"When He, the Spirit of truth, has come, He will guide you into all truth; for He will not speak on His own authority, but whatever He hears He will speak; and He will tell you things to come."

When we accept the Holy Spirit, we are then partnered with the person of God who was sent to give us a behind-the-scenes look and tell us of things to come (see Matthew 28:19 and 1 John 5:7). Because of the Holy Spirit, we can have a relationship with God that looks something like that of Moses, Abraham, and Jesus!

I was going through a very dark season of my life. My dreams were crumbling around me, no matter how desperately I grasped at them. No amount of work, sweat, tears, or prayers seemed to be bringing them back together. I needed a miracle, but I didn't see one anywhere.

During that time, Pastor Robert taught a series called *From Dream to Destiny*. As he unpacked the life of Joseph, I saw parallels to my own life and struggles. I decided that I had to have that book! On my way home from soccer practice (professional soccer was my dream), I drove to the church to see if I could buy it from the bookstore.

Have you ever been in a place where you wanted to shout, "God, I need You now!"? Like you can't go one more moment without some new revelation or a fresh perspective? That's where I was. But as I drove up to the building, I could see the bookstore was closed. I was crushed.

Then the thought (or maybe it was a feeling) came: *Maybe I should go in anyway.* I walked in, and the first person I saw was Pastor Robert's daughter, Elaine. I must have been a sweaty (and probably smelly) sight since I had just come from practice, but she was kind enough to say hi and ask how I was doing. I told her that I was trying to buy *From Dream to Destiny* but didn't realize the bookstore would be closed.

Her response surprised me: "My dad has a ton of those in his garage. Follow me in your car, and we'll get one!" As we drove away from the church, I shook my head in amazement and thought, *God, what are You doing?!*

We arrived at Pastor Robert's house, and Elaine went inside. A few moments later, she returned with a copy of the book, signed by her dad. I couldn't believe it!

The exciting part of this story isn't that I got a signed copy of the book (even though that was definitely special). The exciting part is that at that moment I knew God saw *me*. I thought about the impression I had to go inside the church even though the bookstore was closed. I prayed, "God, help me remember what that felt like because I know now that was You speaking to me." Hearing God changed everything for me in that moment.

When I think about hearing God, I think about the word *necessity*. It's necessary. It's vital. It's crucial to living life well as a friend of God (John 10:10). Isaiah 30:21 promises,

> Your ears shall hear a word behind you, saying,
> "This *is* the way, walk in it,"
> Whenever you turn to the right hand
> or whenever you turn to the left.

But what if you don't have that voice? How will you know which way to turn? I remember a conversation with a friend years ago in which he expressed frustration with his relationship with God. I remember him telling me, "Relationships are supposed to have two-way communication, but I don't hear God! I do all of the talking!" He could not have been more accurate.

There seems to be a gap for many people between knowing they should have a relationship with God and actually having a relationship with Him. I think we've all wondered *How do I get there?* It's not an instant process. Like a baby learning to crawl or walk, it takes time, trial, and plenty of error. I encourage you to start today on your own path of learning to hear God's voice (or learning to hear it better). Maybe you need to read *Frequency*, take a class, or find a mentor who already knows how to hear God. My prayer is that by the end of this book, you will know God's voice better than you did before.

When I was a little boy, I would go to school and meet a cute girl with a cool book bag and nice hair. I would come home and say, "Mom, Dad, there's a cute girl in my class." My mom would respond, "Did you talk to her?" The answer was almost always a bashful, "No ..."

She would encourage me to talk to this girl, so I would. The next day I would muster my courage, and say, "HEY!" I would come home and have the following conversation:

Mom: "Did you talk to her today?"
Me: "Yep!" (spoken proudly)
Mom: "What did you say?"
Me: "I said, 'Hey.'"
Mom: "And what did she say?"
Me: "Um ..."

(You see, at that point in the conversation with the "cute girl", I said my "Hey" and ran off.)

Mom: "Honey, you need to wait and see what she says back."

Over the course of years and much coaching, I began to learn the art of effective communication. It is true for relationships with "cute girls with cool book bags and nice hair," and it's true for our relationship with God as well. We need to learn and be coached on how to hear God. It can take a little time, but it is amazingly necessary to live this life well. It's necessary to get past fear.

―――

We need to learn and be coached on how to hear God.

Reason Three: Your faith depends on it.

When I was nine, I often didn't know what was going on. I didn't worry too much about it, though. Whenever I didn't understand, I filled in the blanks on my own by creating stories. I had answers to all kinds of questions, such as *where do clouds come from?* and *what do dogs say when they howl?*

Gaps such as these are innocent enough for a nine-year-old to fill in. The combination of time and education can rectify most of them without much event. But, on occasion, we find our nine-year-old selves in a situation where we must fill in a blank, and it changes the course of our lives.

There once was a girl named Jane. Jane never knew her father. Each and every birthday, she waited for him to arrive. She hoped and waited and prayed that he would come. Year after year, he let her down.

At nine years old, she couldn't understand why he wouldn't come. But it didn't matter because this next year would be different. Next year she would be 10 years old! That was a big girl birthday. She decided, "I'm not just going to hope—I'm going to have faith that he will come!" She prayed and prayed all year and put all her faith into her father coming for her birthday.

The night before the big day, Jane could barely sleep. Excitement and fear took turns dancing in her mind. She played the movie of what could be over and over and over.

Morning came, and Jane watched the clock slowly move. Tick tock. Tick tock. Her party came and went, and as she sat in the darkness of evening, each car that drove by without stopping was a disappointing reminder that her father wouldn't come. Once again, like every year before, reality crushed her hope. What had happened? Did God let her down? Did she not have enough faith?

Romans 10:17 tells us, "So then faith *comes* by hearing, and hearing by the word of God." Faith requires hearing. What does that mean? **If you haven't heard, then it isn't faith.**

———

If you haven't heard, then it isn't faith.

If you haven't heard, you might just be operating in the hope of what *could* be. If you haven't heard, it could just be wishful thinking. Because without hearing, it isn't faith.

Maybe you have been in the same position as little Jane. You believed God for something big. You wanted it. You wanted it so badly in fact that you decided you would have enough faith to make it happen.

I know God will never fail me or leave me (Deuteronomy 31:6). I know He never lets the righteous fall (Psalm 37:24). The Bible says God will never let me down, but let's be honest: at times, I have felt like He did. Because of hurts and disappointments in my life, I spent years questioning if God really does come through. Those experiences served as a lens through which I gazed at God and reflected back this message: God will let you down.

After talking to God about it and recognizing that His Truth is supreme above even my experience, I had to conclude that even in that moment, God didn't let me down. He didn't let Jane down either. So what happened?

Ultimately, I don't know all that happened in Jane's life, but from my limited perspective, I have to draw the conclusion that perhaps Jane didn't hear. And because she didn't hear, she didn't step out in faith. She stepped out in something else.

Now, before you condemn Jane (or me for drawing this conclusion), please realize that all of us are all learning to hear God better. We are all growing and learning in regard to our relationship with God. Many times I have assigned the word "faith" to my wants in order to try to bend God's arm.

However, the truth remains: without hearing, it's not faith. It may be my desire, hope, and greatest wish, but it's not faith.

———

Without hearing, it's not faith. It may be my desire, hope, and greatest wish, but it's not faith.

Imagine you have lost your job. You have been looking for new employment for months. Multiple places in Scripture tell us that God is our provider. Genesis 22:14 even gives us a name for God our Provider: *Jehovah Jireh.*

And Abraham called the name of the place, The-Lord-Will-Provide; as it is said to this day, "In the Mount of the Lord it shall be provided" Genesis 22:14.

You know and believe this, so when your next interview goes well, you declare, "I have faith that this is the job for me. In fact, I know this is the job for me. By faith, I claim this job!"

Well, that's all good and exciting, but did God speak it? Did God say this job is the job for you? If He has said in His Word that He will provide for you (which He has), then you can put your faith in that. You can say that no matter what happens, no matter if you get this job or another job six months from now, God is your provider and will never let you down. But if He hasn't said that this particular job is yours, you cannot say that you have faith, because you haven't heard. Make sense?

Sometimes we decide that something should be a certain way, so we call our belief "faith" and place an expectation on God. Then when God doesn't meet this expectation, we feel let down, hurt, and confused.

Our God is a good Father. I try to be one too. My daughter knows that I will do everything in my power to keep her from going hungry. Let's say she asks me for ice cream for dinner. This request comes with an expectation that I will give her the ice cream because I know she's hungry. However, I tell my daughter, "No ice cream for dinner." Am I trying to be mean? Not at all. I'm not trying to let her down or frustrate her. It's simply that (a) I cannot give her something that isn't healthy for dinner, even though she thinks it's good and expects it from me, and (b) I cannot train my three-year-old child to think that I will fulfill whatever expectations she places on me. That would place her in the position of control, and at her age, she needs to know that I am the authority.

So it is with God. Sometimes we place expectations on Him of what we should get from His hand, but those things are often the life equivalents of ice cream for dinner. By giving them to us, God might ruin the nutritious dinner that is actually good for us. And He would be training us to believe every expectation placed on Him will be fulfilled (even if it's not for our best). God is a good Father, and He is the ultimate authority. He is the only one who is really in control. He doesn't want us to live in the fantasy land that we are.

———

> He is the only one who is really in control. He doesn't want us to live in the fantasy land that we are.

As we've established, faith comes by hearing. If we take the time to hear, God will speak and say, "Yes." Or He will speak and say, "No." Our part is to hear.

Hearing. Is. Everything.

4

FAITH

Now faith is the substance of things hoped for, the evidence of things not seen.

—Hebrews 11:1

What Is Faith?

I have often heard that faith is the opposite of fear. If this is the case, we must first understand faith if we are going to understand fear.

It's my experience that definitions drift. Like unanchored wood on the shore, they move farther and farther away from their place of origin. The problem with this drifting is that we structure our lives around the meaning of words. Words such as "love," "hope," "belief," and "faith" all serve as pillars in our lives. We can spend our whole lives chasing "success," only to find out that we defined success incorrectly. Devastation, brokenness, and severe disappointment often follow as our pursuit ends in emptiness.

It makes me think of my parents' detached garage. When we first moved into that home in the 1990s, I was beyond excited! Dreams of what could be done showered my mind like confetti at a party! My favorite thing to do was to share those ideas, so I shared one of my best ideas with my dad: "We could add a second story to the garage and have an apartment up there!"

I'm not sure if I was looking for a cool hideout, or if I was secretly hoping that we could rent it out for a profit, but his answer destroyed my dreams of adventure and financial gain. He explained to me that the structure was a little bit off. You couldn't see it from the outside, but if you were to try to add the weight of a second level to the structure, it wouldn't hold. Because of this, the building couldn't reach any further potential than it already had.

This is true in our lives in a profound way. When we build our lives on definitions that are a little bit off, you might not be able to tell from the outside, but your structure won't be able to carry the weight of your full potential. You'll miss out on what could be.

Because of this, like all words that we must define properly, we must define faith correctly. We structure so much of our lives on what we believe faith to be; therefore, we must be sure to define it the right way. Romans 10:17 tells us faith comes from hearing. But *what* is faith?

In college, I studied mathematics quite a bit, and I often found myself facing a dreaded foe: word problems. In case you haven't studied math in a while, word problems sound like a story with a problem. You have to find all the pieces necessary within the story to solve the problem. What makes them difficult is that the pieces are not always obvious. Here's an example:

Todd and Bill were running a race. Todd's shoes weighed 30% more than Bill's shoes. Bill was running the 50-mile race 0.13% faster than Todd. How much stronger is Bill than Todd given that they have comparable body composition dimensions?

Confusing, right? (Don't bother trying to solve that problem, by the way). My point is that word problems are like life's problems: they often seem as if they require a secret to solve. Part of the secret is understanding keywords, which clue you into what is happening in the problem. One keyword is "is." "Is" tells us that there is an equal sign. Did you know there is an equal sign in Hebrews 11:1? This verse says, "Faith is ..." This can be translated into "Faith = ___." What does faith equal? According to the verse, faith = "the substance of things hoped for, the evidence of things not seen." Great! But what does that actually mean?

———

Faith = "the substance of things hoped for, the evidence of things not seen."

Allow me to answer that question with another: How can you know God will ever do anything in your life? How can you know He ever has?

I went to Egypt for the first time in 2010. While there, I got very sick. Lying in bed, unable to eat, and burning with fever, I slipped in and out of consciousness. Of course, the enemy decided he'd come in and kick me while I was down. Each time I awoke, I had a mental movie of every time God did something in my life. However, these movies were versions that attempted to show me how every interaction and experience I had ever had with God was false. These visions, if you will, were trying to make me let go of the only thing that I could wholly put my hope in: God.

I struggled and struggled, unable to come up with arguments to fight the movies. The only word I could find was "no." I couldn't argue my way through the enemy's arguments. I could only hold onto the single shred of faith that I could find. I had heard God in my life. I knew He was real. I would hold onto that.

You can only hold onto something of substance. If you have hope with no faith, you have nothing to hold onto. You have no guarantee that what you hope for will ever come to pass.

How do you hope for something? You hope for something when you have heard of it. You don't even know to put your hope in a better tomorrow unless you have heard that tomorrow could be better.

Faith comes by hearing, and faith is the thing that you can hold onto. You have placed your trust in the One who has told you that there is something to hope for.

When my daughter puts her faith in me, it's because I've told her something that she can hope toward. If I tell her, "We'll get ice cream in a minute," she can tell doubters, "I am going to have ice cream because my daddy said so." She puts her faith in me and can hold onto that faith because I won't disappoint her.

Faith is trusting that what someone has said is true. You can hold onto it in a real, substantial way. It's like buying a train ticket for the west. The ticket is the thing that I can hold onto because I trust the one who told me that it would get me west. My hope is in going west; my faith is in the ticket. I can't hold my hope, but I can hold my faith. I've heard, and I believe it.

This is an important reason why we first examined hearing. In order to have faith, you hear first. If you haven't heard, you cannot have faith. If you don't have faith (if you don't trust what God said to be true), you may never overcome fear.

Before we move on, I have to make this point: faith comes by hearing, *not* by understanding. You may be waiting to put your faith in God until after you understand why things are the way they are. You may have had something confusing, hurtful, or terrible happen, and you've told yourself, "I'll believe God in this area once I can figure this out."

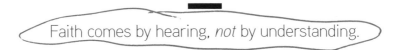

Faith comes by hearing, *not* by understanding.

If you're waiting to understand to have faith, you may end up waiting until it's too late. Faith comes by *hearing*. Ask God to speak to you today. Ask Him, "Are you really faithful?" Expect an answer. God is ready to speak—He is ready for you to have faith.

Why Is Faith Important?

Have you ever heard the phrase "by faith"? Those are some powerful words. In Hebrews 11, the writer refers us back to Genesis 12 and makes sure we know that Abraham acted "by faith" (see verses 8–10). Abraham is often referred to as the father of our faith, but when did this faith start?

It started when Abraham was still called "Abram." As we read in chapter 1, God told Abram to leave everything he had ever known and go to the place "that I will show you." Abram heard, and his faith was born.

Each milestone of Abraham's life is listed in Hebrews 11 as having been done "by faith":

By faith Abraham obeyed when he was called to go out to the place which he would receive as an inheritance. And he went out, not knowing where he was going. By faith he dwelt in the land of promise as *in* a foreign country, dwelling in tents with Isaac and Jacob, the heirs with him of the same promise; for he waited for the city which has foundations, whose builder and maker *is* God (vv. 8–10).

By faith Abraham, when he was tested, offered up Isaac, and he who had received the promises offered up his only begotten *son*, of whom it was said, "In Isaac your seed shall be called," concluding that God was able to raise *him* up, even from the dead, from which he also received him in a figurative sense (vv. 17–19).

The importance of faith is multifaceted, but here are three reasons why faith is important for our own life journeys:

Faith carries us forward in the face of adversity.

By faith, Abraham stepped out into the unknown. It was an unknown that spoke against him in every way. How do I know? Because a similar unknown spoke against me. I know that it has spoken against you.

The voice comes against you in those times when the stakes are high and the future is questionable. When my professional soccer dreams ended, my future was a desert. I didn't know what was ahead, but a voice was present to tell me of all that could be—and it wasn't pretty. That voice was fear. I'm thankful that my faith in my God was stronger than my fear; it allowed me to move forward.

Abraham's faith allowed him to move forward too. He moved forward to a foreign country with no allies and no friends. He was completely dependent upon God. Abraham moved up the mountain with sticks for a fire and his son.

How could he offer Isaac—his beloved child and the divinely promised heir—as a sacrifice to God? Who would do such a thing? A man with faith, that's who.

Sometimes hope is for something great. Other times hope looks forward and tells us that all isn't going to be well. In Romans 4:18, Paul writes about Abraham, "Who, contrary to hope, in hope believed, so that he became the father of many nations, according to what was spoken, 'So shall your descendants be.'"

Abram hoped against hope. He was so old that he was as good as dead, yet he *still* had hope that God would deliver on his promises.

> And not being weak in faith, he did not consider his own body, already dead (since he was about a hundred years old), and the deadness of Sarah's womb. He did not waver at the promise of God through unbelief, but was strengthened in faith, giving glory to God, and being fully convinced that what He had promised He was also able to perform. And therefore "it was accounted to him for righteousness" (Romans 4:19–22).

Faith keeps us moving forward in the face of opposition, even when opposition sounds like logic. Logic told Abraham, "You're old. God hasn't shown up, so give up." Human "logic" is often a disguise for the voice of the enemy. The greatest true logic is to believe that the God who holds all things in His hands is limited by nothing (not even time) and can deliver on the promises that *He* makes in *His* time.

Faith keeps us moving forward in the face of opposition, even when opposition sounds like logic.

You will experience adversity in this life. Jesus said we would: "In the world you will have tribulation" (John 16:33). This leads us to the second reason faith is important:

You must have faith to get past this issue of fear.

Fear is going to sound right some of the time. You have to be able to look at the facts that are offered to you and then think back on what God has told you. You have to be able to look to God and, even if you are too hurt, beat up, and swollen to remember the words, remember your faith in Him. It's the only way that you will be able to hope against hope. It's the only way that you will be free of the fear that binds you.

———

> You have to be able to look to God and, even if you are too hurt, beat up, and swollen to remember the words, remember your faith in Him.

You cannot please God without hearing Him.

You can't just read the Bible like a rule book and perform the rules well enough to please God. I've tried that, and it didn't work for me. The Pharisees tried it, and it didn't work for them. Paul, the Pharisee of Pharisees, couldn't do it either (Philippians 3:2–7). We all need Jesus.

Hebrews 11:6 tells us, "Without faith *it is* impossible to please *Him*, for he who comes to God must believe that He is, and *that* He is a rewarder of those who diligently seek Him."

If faith comes by hearing, and you cannot please God without faith, then it is certainly impossible to please God without first hearing His voice.

If faith comes by hearing, and you cannot please God without faith, then it is certainly impossible to please God without first hearing His voice.

The only way we can truly please God is to put our faith and trust in Jesus Christ. The Holy Spirit is drawing you to God. You will never get there if you don't pause long enough to hear His invitation to trust Him. Put your faith in who He is. Put your faith in His ability to be bigger, stronger, and more powerful than anything that can come against you. Jesus doesn't leave us without hope:

"In the world you will have tribulation; but be of good cheer, I have overcome the world" (John 16:33).

5

FEAR AND OBEDIENCE

And Abraham stretched out his hand and took the knife to slay his son.

—Genesis 22:10

Growing up I wasn't much of a social person. I would go to parties with friends, which sounds very social, but most of the memories I have are of furniture legs and people's shoes. I would walk around with my eyes cast down, avoiding eye contact.

I feared people. I feared rejection and the possibility of embarrassment. So if the fear of rejection told me to look down, I did. If the fear of failure told me not to volunteer to work on a project, I didn't. If it told me to leave a room, I did. And if it told me not to talk to someone, you can be assured that I didn't talk to them! I obeyed what I feared in every area of my life.

Jeremiah 5:22–23 says,

"Do you not fear Me?" says the Lord.
"Will you not tremble at My presence,
Who have placed the sand as the bound of the sea,
By a perpetual decree, that it cannot pass beyond it?
And though its waves toss to and fro,
Yet they cannot prevail;

Though they roar, yet they cannot pass over it.
But this people has a defiant and rebellious heart;
They have revolted and departed."

Here in these verses, God describes His people as having defiant, rebellious hearts and not fearing Him. They revolted and departed from Him. They didn't fear Him, and they certainly didn't obey Him.

At King Saul's coronation, the prophet Samuel said,

"If you fear the Lord and serve Him and obey His voice, and do not rebel against the commandment of the Lord, then both you and the king who reigns over you will continue following the Lord your God" (I Samuel 12:14).

It's simple: what you fear, you obey. Fear comes before obedience. If you obey the voice in your head that tells you to do whatever it takes to make someone like you, you probably fear rejection. If you obey the voice in your head that tells you to lie about how you are doing, you likely struggle with trust. "What you fear, you obey" is one of the reasons I believe God emphasizes obeying Him so much throughout Scripture. He knows that obedience points toward fear.

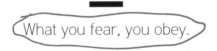

What you fear, you obey.

When the people of Israel were in bondage to Egypt, Pharaoh commanded the Hebrew midwives to kill all the male newborn babies. But the midwives refused. Why? They "feared God, and did not do as the king of Egypt commanded them, but saved the male children alive" (Exodus 1:17). The midwives could not obey Pharaoh's command because they didn't fear him. They feared God, so they were going to be obedient to His commands. A blessing came from their fear-motivated obedience: "And so it was, because the midwives feared God, that He provided households for them" (Exodus 1:21).

As people, we don't always see obedience as much of a priority as God does. We want to chase the blessing, but we don't always chase obedience.

———

> We want to chase the blessing,
> but we don't always chase obedience.

One of the appeals of my professional soccer dream was that I would be a big deal and that I would make a big deal about Jesus. It was a win-win. I would be rich and famous, and, in turn, I would make God famous as I changed the world in His name.

As my soccer dream fell apart, so did my opportunity to become rich and famous. My chance to be a big deal and make a big deal of God diminished. I felt my big impact for God slipping away.

After soccer ended, every other door that closed in my face seemed to emphasize that reality. Whether it was business, acting, or anything in between, each closed door seemed to make my window of impacting the world for Jesus shrink even smaller.

One day, after a series of closed doors, I called a good friend of mine. You always can tell a good friend from a bad friend because a bad friend will sometimes tell you what makes you feel good. A good friend, however, will tell you what is good for you, no matter how it feels.

Looking at my situation, and not seeing much of a chance to impact the world for God, I exclaimed in frustration, "I just want to make a difference in this world for God!"

Don't we all? Doesn't every good, believing, Jesus-following Christian want to have an impact on our world? No one truly grasps the gravity of what Jesus did for them and then turns around and says, "I'm so glad I got that out of the way. Now I'll hide under a rock." The joy and gratitude of being saved from sin and eternal separation from our Heavenly Father are more than one can contain!

That day on the phone, my friend didn't tell me to try harder. He didn't tell me to be brave and dig in my heels into the dirt. Instead, he calmly said, "Benjamin, God doesn't ask you to make a difference. He asks you to be obedient."

God doesn't ask you to make a difference. He asks you to be obedient.

Those words fell on me like a hammer. The truth of their correction landed on my chest like a comforting weight. They washed me of the pressure of ambition, took away my need to perform, and set me on a path to hear what God was actually asking me to do.

My friend's correction reminded me of 1 Samuel 15. Samuel found Saul doing "great" things, but these things were *not* what God had told the king to do. Samuel said,

> Has the Lord *as great* delight in burnt offerings and sacrifices,
> As in obeying the voice of the Lord?

Behold, to obey is better than sacrifice,
And to heed than the fat of rams (v. 22)

God looks for obedience because obedience shows what
you fear. What do you fear?

> God looks for obedience because
> obedience shows what you fear.

We know from Hebrews 11:8 that Abraham obeyed God
by faith when He called him to go out to a land that he didn't
know. Then, years later, God asked Abraham to sacrifice Isaac.
The father didn't make half-hearted plans or pretend to obey.
He built an altar, tied up his son, and raised the knife to kill
him. Only when Abraham was willing to give up that which he
cherished most did God interrupt and say, "Now I know that
you fear God" (Genesis 22:12). Abraham's extreme obedience
was a sign of his fear. Abraham feared God, so he obeyed Him.
What you fear, you obey!

Over the years, I have been guilty of obeying quite a few
voices, many of which were based in fear. I feared someone
breaking into my house, so I would check multiple times that
the doors were locked before going to bed. I feared my wife
dying, so with her permission, I would track her on my phone.
I feared; therefore, I obeyed.

If you aren't obeying God, you might be fearing something
else. James 2:20-21 says,

But do you want to know, O foolish man, that faith without
works is dead? Was not Abraham our father justified by
works when he offered Isaac his son on the altar?

When we obey and act upon the voice speaking to us, we put works into action. Those works partner with our faith and do something. When we obey God, we partner faith and works, and the result is justification. Romans 10:9–10 tells us,

> If you confess with your mouth the Lord Jesus and believe in your heart that God has raised Him from the dead, you will be saved. For with the heart one believes unto righteousness, and with the mouth confession is made unto salvation.

———

When we obey God, we partner faith and works, and the result is justification.

When you put your faith in God and confess Jesus as your Lord, you are saved! There is no greater display of faith and works partnered for justification.

When Pharaoh saw that his plan to eradicate the Hebrews' male babies was foiled, he went for a new plan.

> Pharaoh commanded all his people, saying, "Every son who is born you shall cast into the river, and every daughter you shall save alive" (Exodus 1:22).

This verse hit me hard recently. I have seen several depictions of the Exodus story over the years, and each one has portrayed Egyptian soldiers killing the male babies. The scenes are chilling. However, Exodus 1:17 paints a different picture for us. This verse tells us that Pharaoh didn't command the soldiers to do this. He commanded the people! How many parents threw their own children into the river?

How many mothers and fathers sacrificed their sons out of fear? It grieves me to think of it.

Acts 7:19 says, "This man dealt treacherously with our people, and oppressed our forefathers, making them expose their babies, so that they might not live." As I think about the atrocity of having to throw your own child into the Nile River, I can't help but reflect on myself and the society within which I live. How many parents today sacrifice their children based on the voice of fear? A fear to fit in. A fear to survive.

One family decided to have a different story:

> By faith Moses, when he was born, was hidden three months by his parents, because they saw he was a beautiful child; and they were not afraid of the king's command (Hebrews 11:23).

Moses' parents didn't fear the king's command. They feared God. And because they feared Him, they obeyed Him.

Whose voice are you obeying? Whom do you fear?

6

IS FEAR GOOD OR BAD?

Blessed *is* the man *who* fears the Lord,
Who delights greatly in His commandments.

Psalm 112:1

When I think of a snake, I think, *That animal will bite your face on your birthday, send you to the hospital, and not even think twice.* Most people would agree that having a fear of snakes is a good idea. No one likes puncture wounds filled with painful or deadly poison.

When we think of fearing success, however, we think, *That's bad. That will cause you to self-sabotage your life and keep you from reaching your full potential.* Here, in this situation, we would all agree that this fear is bad.

Through these two scenarios, we see a duality to fear. It's almost as if fear has two faces. Is fear good, or is it bad?

I was raised in church. Actually, I was raised in several churches, each having its own focus on certain things within God's Word and the world around us. Some things were consistent, like who Jesus is. Another common teaching was that fear is bad. Those sermons resonated within me because of my own life experiences. I didn't take much convincing to agree: fear is *bad*.

To emphasize the sermons about how bad fear was, there was the slogan "Fear not!" I can still see those words plastered on bumper stickers and t-shirts in the community I grew up in. After all, fear isn't of God. Fear will hold us back from all that God wants for us in this abundant life He promises. Right?

I avoided fear like the plague. My friends in youth group, on the other hand, constantly went to see scary movies. I knew they had heard the same sermons I did, and some of them even wore the cheesy t-shirts. So why would they purposely invite fear into their lives? It seemed counterintuitive and foolish, almost like taking advantage of God. I mean, if fear is bad, why would you open the door to it?

So there I was, walking through life and feeling like a man on a mission, with my "try-real-hard" gear in full-throttle, saying, "I will not fear" (all the while fighting fear quite poorly). Then, without warning, I was thrown a curve ball. It came as a realization that what the church had been telling me all of my life was somehow hitting up against Scripture telling me to fear God! What!? Is God scary?

But it wasn't just the church telling me this. No, the same Bible that I read all of my life backed this seemingly contradictory idea! The same Bible that told me to "fear not" also told me to "fear God."

> "You are not to say, 'It is a conspiracy!'
> In regard to all that this people call a conspiracy,
> And you are not to fear what they fear or be in dread of it.
> It is the Lord of hosts whom you should regard as holy.
> And He shall be your fear,
> And He shall be your dread" (Isaiah 8:12–13 NASB).

Not convinced that we should fear God? Jesus, our perfect example—the one we are to follow—feared God! Prophesying about the coming Messiah, Isaiah says,

> The Spirit of the Lord will rest on Him,
> The spirit of wisdom and understanding,
> The spirit of counsel and strength,
> The spirit of knowledge and the fear of the Lord
> (Isaiah 11:12).

When I first read that verse, it felt like my brain fell apart. Jesus *feared* God?

Here we find ourselves at a crossroads. What do we do with the command to fear not and the other command to fear God? The seemingly conflicting ideas must cause us to pause. They are a paradox that cause many individuals, and even denominations, to leap to a decision.

It seems to me that at this pivotal crossroad of understanding fear, we often choose one of these conclusions:

1. "Fearing God" was for the Old Testament and doesn't apply today, so we should just "fear not."
2. "Fearing God" is biblical because of the Old Testament, so we can't avoid it; it's still around and applicable. Look at how He destroyed people in the Old Testament! Look at how He destroyed Ananias and Sapphira in Acts 5 for lying about their giving! From this we can conclude that yes, we should fear God because He can destroy us. We need to watch out and just forget the whole "fear not" idea.
3. Fearing God is simply respecting or revering Him, much like how you revere or respect your parents. The fear that God tells us *not* to have is a different kind of fear from the fear that we are *supposed* to have for God.

However, I have a problem with each of these conclusions.

Problem with Conclusion 1

The Old Testament wasn't erased with the New Testament. Jesus didn't come to do away with the Law; He came to fulfill it (Matthew 5:17–20). Because of this, you cannot dismiss the idea of "fearing God" presented in the Old Testament. In addition, this argument that "fearing God appears in the Old Testament" doesn't nullify the fact that fearing God also appears in the New Testament.

> "And His mercy *is* on those who **fear Him**
> From generation to generation" (Luke 1:50, emphasis added).

When Jesus came to fulfill the law, He actually called us to deeper righteousness in Him. He didn't do away with it.

> "You have heard that it was said to those of old, You shall not murder, and whoever murders will be in danger of the judgment.' But I say to you that whoever is angry with his brother without a cause shall be in danger of the judgment. And whoever says to his brother, 'Raca!' shall be in danger of the council. But whoever says, 'You fool!' shall be in danger of hell fire.... You have heard that it was said to those of old, 'You shall not commit adultery.' But I say to you that whoever looks at a woman to lust for her has already committed adultery with her in his heart (Matthew 5:21–22, 27–28).

Jesus calls us to higher living. It's a living that we can only achieve through the power of the Holy Spirit. We can't achieve it with works.

Jesus calls us to higher living. It's a living that
we can only achieve through the power of
the Holy Spirit. We can't achieve it with works.

"Not by might nor by power, but by My Spirit"
Says the Lord of hosts (Zechariah 4:6).

Could it be that Jesus is calling us also to fear God at new
levels?

Problem with Conclusion 2

I know people who were raised in a church environment
where fearing God was synonymous with fearing God's wrath
/punishment. "Don't do anything wrong, or God will strike
you down!" They were told that a good relationship with Him
equated to doing all of the right things in just the right way and
avoiding all of the bad things. If you messed up, you must pay
for it with the right prayers, said the right way, the right amount
of times. If you did EXACTLY what you were told, you could
avoid that certain, looming punishment we all fear: destruction
by God's hand. It is a tiring lifestyle. It is unsustainable.

I lived much of my life this way: trying to earn God's love
and avoiding His displeasure. I worked and worked and tried
and tried to be good enough. The result: I was constantly
judging others who didn't measure up to my performance
yardstick, and I was always looking over my shoulder, trying to
be good enough but failing. It was miserable.

Fearing God's ability to strike us down based upon our
behavior doesn't leave much room for the grace that Jesus
brought into the picture. While we are not ignorant of God's

power and the consequences associated with disobedience, fearing God in this way seems to miss the mark.

———

Fearing God's ability to strike us down based upon our behavior doesn't leave much room for the grace that Jesus brought into the picture.

Living under the belief that to fear God is to fear His ability to destroy us abandons the truth that God sent Jesus to save the world, not condemn it (John 3:17); that He Himself is love (1 John 4:8); and that He is full of grace (John 1:14). His wrath was poured out on Jesus, and He offers us salvation through His Son (1 Thessalonians 5:9).

In Acts 5, Ananias and Sapphira lie about how much money they sold their land for so they could keep some for themselves. Because they lie to the Holy Spirit, they both die. The result of this event was that "great fear came over the whole church" (Acts 5:11).

It's hard to wrap my mind around that story. How do I reconcile it with a God who is full of love and grace? I don't think God wants us to run for cover every time we mess up (much like Adam and Eve did in Genesis 3:8).

Baker Encyclopedia of the Bible eloquently states that fear is "often spoken of as the source of religion. Yet fear alone can never account for true religion, since men are compelled to draw near unto God, the object of their worship. One does not desire to come close to the being he fears."[6]

---

6. S. D. Sacks, *Baker Encyclopedia of the Bible, vol. 1* (Grand Rapids, MI: Baker Book House, 1988), s.v. "Fear."

Problem with Conclusion 3

One issue I have with defining "fearing God" solely as "reverence or respect" is that while the definition may be correct under certain circumstances, it does not fully encapsulate the definition of fear across the whole of Scripture (we'll get into this more later).

Ephesians 5:21 tells us, "And be subject to one another in the **fear of Christ**" (NASB, emphasis added). Fear of Christ? But He died for me. He loves me. So why would I fear Him? The Greek word used for fear in this verse is *phobos*, from which we derive "phobia."

Don't believe me? It's true! Jesus made people afraid all the time! When He healed a paralytic and forgave his sins, the crowds reacted this way:

> They marveled and glorified God, who had given such power to men (Matthew 9:8).

The Greek word for "marveled" in this passage is, again, *phobeo*.

Even the disciples feared Jesus! One evening they were crossing the lake when a terrible storm threatened to capsize their boat.

> And they came to Him [Jesus] and awoke Him, saying, "Master, Master, we are perishing!"
>
> Then He arose and rebuked the wind and the raging of the water. And they ceased, and there was a calm. But He said to them, "Where is your faith?"
>
> And they were **afraid**, and marveled, saying to one another, "Who can this be? For He commands even the winds and water, and they obey Him!" (Luke 8:24-25, emphasis added).

Don't worry ... it gets even more confusing. We read in 1 John 4:18, "There is no fear in love; but perfect love casts out fear, because fear involves punishment, and the one who fears is not perfected in love." According to this verse, perfect love drives out fear! How is it that I'm supposed to fear God who is the very source of love? The only reason we even know love is because "He first loved us" (1 John 1:19).

Look at Job: "There was a man in the land of Uz whose name was Job; and that man was blameless, upright, fearing God and turning away from evil" (Job 1:1 NASB). Job was a good guy. He lived a good life according to how God would measure and define good. He feared God. Well done Job!

But Job's story takes a surprising turn:

> The LORD said to Satan, "Have you considered My servant Job? For there is no one like him on the earth, a blameless and upright man, fearing God and turning away from evil." Then Satan answered the LORD, "Does Job fear God for nothing? Have You not made a hedge about him and his house and all that he has, on every side? You have blessed the work of his hands, and his possessions have increased in the land. But put forth Your hand now and touch all that he has; he will surely curse You to Your face" (Job 1:8-11).

Satan says that Job fears God because of all of the good that God has given him. Now, we can't trust anything Satan says because he's the father of lies, but this statement is very confusing to me and cannot be ignored (because God left it in Scripture and did not correct Satan). How could someone fear God because of the *good* God has given them? If anything, I thought that we could possibly fear God because He might destroy us!

Exodus 20:20 sums up this confusion in one little verse:

Moses said to the people, "**Do not be afraid**; for God has come in order to test you, and in order that the **fear of Him may remain with you**, so that you may not sin" (emphasis added).

There it is in one verse. The ultimate contradiction: fear not; fear God.

In an effort to get some light shed upon this conundrum, I looked at the original languages that the Text was written in (Greek and Hebrew). Maybe this would be the key to helping me understand how I am to "fear God" and "fear not" at the same time.

My first thought was that maybe the words in Hebrew and Greek that we have translated for "fear" are different when referring to God than when referring to our enemies. However, this isn't the case.

- "Fear of Christ" (Ephesians 5:21 NASB) is the same fear as "fear of her [Babylon's] torment" (Revelation 18:15 NASB) and the same as "fear" of God when Ananias and Sapphira were killed.
- "Do not fear, Abram, / I am a shield to you" (Genesis 15:1 NASB) or "I will fear no evil" (Psalm 23:4) is the same fear as "You shall fear *only* the LORD your God" (Deuteronomy 6:13 NASB).

Looking for answers, I began to study. I looked up all of the Hebrew and Greek words for fear in the Bible to see if they would shed light on this mystery. Here they are:

HEBREW

יִרְאָה yirah: fear

יָרֵא yare: fearful; in fear of; to fear; be afraid; to fear God; to
be feared, be honored; dreaded

פַּחַד pachad: dread; to shiver; tremble; to be startled, be in
terror

מוֹרָה morah: fear; awe; terror

גּוּר gur: to be afraid

עָרַץ arats: to terrify

מְגוֹרָה megorah: object of dread, horror[7]

GREEK

φόβος phobos: fear

φοβέω phobeō: be afraid; be cowardly

ἀφόβως aphobōs: fearlessly; without fear

πτόησις ptoēsis: terrified

δειλιάω deiliaō: to be cowardly[8]

As you can imagine, I looked at this list, how we interpret
each of these words as "fear" in English, and how many
of them are used in seemingly contradictory instances
(as exampled above), and I was confused!

I talked to my friend who was raised in Israel and who
speaks and reads Hebrew. He said, "It's all fear to me." He

---

7. William L. Holladay, Ludwig Koehler, and Walter Baumgartner, A
Concise Hebrew and Aramaic Lexicon of the Old Testament: Based
upon the Lexical Work of Ludwig Koehler and Walter Baumgartner
(Leiden: Brill, 2000).

8. James Swanson, A Dictionary of Biblical Languages with Semantic
Domains: Greek (New Testament) (electronic ed.). (Logos Research
Systems, Inc., 1997).

wasn't even sure how they get all of their translation options into English. I was like, "You're no help to me!"

"Okay!" You exclaim in exhaustion. "What's the answer?! Is fear good, or is fear bad?"

Please allow me to suggest a fourth conclusion as an alternative to the other three.

CONCLUSION 4: Fear is neither good nor bad!

What if fear is neutral? What if it only becomes good or bad because we attach it to good or bad things?

Imagine fear as a tree.

If a fear tree is planted in negative soil, it will produce negative fruit. A great man once wrote, "Fear freezes the spontaneity of life. The more fear there is in us, the less alive we are." And according to Max Lucado, "Fear, mismanaged, leads to sin. Sin leads to hiding. Since we've all sinned, we all hide, not in bushes, but in eighty-hour work weeks, temper tantrums, and religious busyness. We avoid contact with

God."[9] A person who eats this negative fruit will grimace, spit it out, and make a mental note: *Fear is the worst! Avoid it at all costs.*

But what if the fear tree is planted in the positive soil of God's Word? Then its fruit will look, smell, and taste like God's promises. Someone who eats will think: *Fear is amazing!*

So why do most people—even Christians—think of fear as a bad thing? I believe it is because we learn at a very early age to fear the wrong things. Fear becomes a negative thing in our lives when we fear things that bring negative by-product and consequences. And once we've learned to see fear as negative, it's very difficult to change our thinking. A pastor can tell us to "fear God," which motivates us to obey the Bible. However, experience has taught us that fear is bad, dangerous even, so we subconsciously transfer that fear is negative over to believing that fearing God is negative. We have trouble imagining a way to fear God other than one that would entail some sort of negative by-product (namely, punishment). We think that fearing God must have to do with something negative like lightning striking us or the earth swallowing us whole!

———

> We have trouble imagining a way to fear God other than one that would entail some sort of negative byproduct (namely, punishment).

Think about all that fear has produced in your life. Maybe fear has left you immobilized or caused you to snap. Perhaps

---

9. *Lucado, Max, Fearless* (Thomas Nelson, 2014).

the fear of rejection has led you to reject others first. Or the fear of failure has kept you from even trying at all.

Then we look at Jesus, and we read how our punishment was poured out on Him. Our minds can't comprehend how to "fear God," because the negative consequence was already bestowed upon His Son. We then look with confusion on the verses that tell us about how great it is for us to fear God.

Here are a few of my favorite (more can be found in Appendix B):

The Lord is a friend to those who fear him.
He teaches them his covenant.
My eyes are always on the Lord,
for he rescues me from the traps of my enemies"
(Psalm 25:14-15 NLT).

Blessed *is* the man *who* fears the Lord,
Who delights greatly in His commandments (Psalm 112:1).

You who fear the Lord, trust in the Lord;
He *is* their help and their shield (Psalm 115:11).

Do not be wise in your own eyes;
Fear the Lord and turn away from evil.
It will be healing to your body
And refreshment to your bones (Proverbs 3:7–8 NASB).

Those who fear the LORD are secure;
he will be a refuge for their children.
Fear of the LORD is a life-giving fountain;
it offers escape from the snares of death
(Proverbs 14:26–27 NLT).

The fear of the Lord *leads* to life,
And *he who has it* will abide in satisfaction;
He will not be visited with evil (Proverbs 19:23).

But to you who fear My name
The Sun of Righteousness shall arise
With healing in His wings (Malachi 4:2).

Here is the truth: when we fear God, the by-products are **positive:** security, safety for our children, life, wisdom, understanding, healing, friendship, refreshment, and so on.

But what about all the verses that tell us not to fear? Here's something that may surprise you: every "do not fear" or "fear not" in Scripture has a direct object (stated or implied) attached to it. What do I mean? Let's look at a simple sentence: "The boy throws the **ball**." In that sentence, "ball" is the direct object.

The direct object is the thing that the action is being applied to directly. Even if that direct object is implied rather than explicitly stated, it is important. I can tell my daughter, "Don't throw the ball" or simply "Don't throw." Either way, she knows I am referring to the ball she's holding in her hand.

It's the same for fear in Scripture. The direct object can be implied or stated. When God told the Israelites "Do not fear," the Israelites knew what He was talking about, whether enemy forces, poverty, or lack of food and water. Interestingly enough, I have not found a blanket verse that only tells us "Do not fear" (without a stated or implied direct object).

We see a great example of an implied direct object in Genesis 15:1:

"After these things the word of the Lord came to Abram in a vision, saying,
'Do not fear, Abram,
I am a shield to you;
Your reward shall be very great.'"

What is Abram not to fear? In Genesis 14 his nephew Lot is kidnapped from Sodom and taken captive. Abram then goes to battle against the captors and defeats them all. Out of gratitude, the King of Sodom offers Abram all the riches of the land. Abram does something interesting, though: he refuses. He declines by saying, "I have sworn to the Lord God Most High, possessor of heaven and earth, that I will not take a thread or a sandal thong or anything that is yours, for fear you would say, 'I have made Abram rich'" (Genesis 14:22–23 NASB).

I can imagine Abram walking away and then shaking his head and thinking, "Man, that was a missed opportunity!" He had a very real chance to fear not having enough; he was walking into a place unknown, led by a God that many didn't know.

You are chained to what you fear. You will look to whatever it is you fear for approval before you move. When we fear the wrong things, we are chained to them and will only be able to go where they allow. When we fear God, we are holding His hand like a child asking if we can go, and He gives us freedom!

———

You are chained to what you fear. You will look to whatever it is you fear for approval before you move.

A friend once said, "I shouldn't fear. God didn't make me to fear." But what if He did?

Let's remember this truth: the enemy created nothing—he only perverts. He perverts love and sexuality. He perverts worship. And he perverts fear.

Colossians 1:16 tells us, "For by Him [Jesus] all things were created that are in heaven and that are on earth, visible and invisible, whether thrones or dominions or principalities or powers. All things were created through Him and for Him." *God created fear.*

Think about that for a minute. Why would God do that?

God created fear so that we could live life well. God created fear so that we could enjoy a full life. Yes, God created fear.

———

God created fear so that we could enjoy a full life.

Okay, so fearing God is good; fearing anything else is bad. Simple enough. But, what is fear and, really, why would God create it?

7

IS FEAR ...

For God has not given us a spirit of fear, but of power and love
and of a sound mind.

—2 Timothy 1:7

An Emotion?

Like a lifeless blob, I stood there. Frozen. Functionless. I
couldn't remember what I was going to say, or even what
words meant. My eyes were wide, my stomach was churning,
and my mouth was as dry as a desert. Panic turned my
thoughts to mush, and fear took center stage in my mind.

Can you relate to a moment like that? Maybe you had to
give a speech or a presentation, and the moment you stepped
on stage, your ears started ringing and your thoughts melted
away into oblivion. If I were to ask you how that situation felt,
you might say "Stressful!"

Fear and stress have an interesting relationship, with similar
results. In his popular book *Boundaries,* Dr. Henry Cloud shares
that fear is an emotional response (like anger) to danger. While
anger causes us to engage in danger, fear causes us to flee from it.[10]

---

10. Henry Cloud and John Townsend, *Boundaries* (Grand Rapids:
Zondervan, 1992).

According to an article in *Psychology Today*, both fear and stress may be classified as emotions.[11] Emotions don't come without consequences. The emotion that we call love can cause us to make decisions that others might label as blind. The emotion of sadness can cause us to disengage and alienate ourselves from community.

Dr. Richard A. Swenson shares in his book *Margin* that some researchers believe fear to be the root cause of all stress reactions. Any stressor (economic vulnerability, loss of control, conditional relationships, overloaded lives, etc.) may find fear at its root.[12]

Research done by the University of Minnesota shows that chronic fear can cause issues in physical health including but not limited to cardiovascular damage, gastro-intestinal problems such as ulcers and irritable bowel syndrome, and decreased fertility. Accelerated aging and even premature death have been documented. That's not all though.

The research also shows that fear can impair the formation of long-term memories and, over time, can decrease the brain's ability to control and regulate fear reactions. This leaves those who fight fear on a regular basis spinning down and out of control. In addition, prolonged fear can affect our ability to read non-verbal cues and other information. This,

---

11. Mary C. Lamia, "The Complexity of Fear," *Psychology Today, December 15,* 2011, accessed November 29, 2018, https://www.psychologytoday.com/us/blog/intense-emotions-and-strong-feelings/201112/the-complexity-fear.

12. Richard A. Swenson, *Margin: How to Create the Emotional, Physical, Financial & Time Reserves You Need* (Colorado Springs: NavPress, 2004.)

in turn, affects our ability to make good decisions and act appropriately.[13]

According to an article in *ScienceDaily*, the same parts of the brain affected by fear relate to stress.[14] Stress and fear overlap. One may even argue without much difficulty that fear is a stressor.

——

The same parts of the brain affected
by fear relate to stress.

So, what's my point? There's a reactionary stress emotion that is incited in the event of perceived danger. This emotion, when left unchecked, will control you. The devastating effects on our mental, emotional, and physical health can be tragically epic. The results of this stress response and its effects present as a mountain that only a faith in something more can break. Here, in these articles, I would again say that the problem isn't the fear—it's the object of fear.

While fear is, in fact, an emotion, we mustn't relegate it to simply that. If fear were but an emotion, it would imply that when we are commanded and invited to fear God, our relationship should be based solely on emotion. It would imply that emotion toward God leads to wisdom, knowledge, and understanding. But our feelings are

13. Sue Towey, "Impact of Fear and Anxiety," Taking Charge of Your Health and Wellbeing, 2016, accessed November 8, 2016, http://www.takingcharge.csh.umn.edu/impact-fear-and-anxiety.
14. Baycrest Centre for Geriatric Care. "Chronic stress, anxiety can damage the brain, increase risk of major psychiatric disorders." ScienceDaily, January 21, 2016, accessed November 8, 2018, http://www.sciencedaily.com/releases/2016/01/160121121818.htm.

wavering. In this context, to fear God would mean we would have to hold a particular emotion always. I don't know about you but holding happiness for an extended period can prove elusive. Emotions change.

If fear were only an emotion, either this book would end here, or the rest of this book would be about how to control emotions, but fear is something more.

A Spirit?

This is a question that seems easily answered on the surface. Second Timothy 1:7 plainly tells us there is a spirit of fear: "For God has not given us a spirit of fear, but of power and love and of a sound mind." In understanding fear as a spirit, we will receive a clue into the strategy and intentions of our ultimate enemy, Satan. We do not want to be ignorant of his schemes (2 Corinthians 2:10–11).

When I was little, I loved stories of medieval times. Tales of brave knights doing good things gave me something to aspire to! These warriors had a higher code of honor, conduct, belief, and loyalty that set them apart from others. I couldn't get enough of the stories of Robin of Loxley (also known as Robin Hood) robbing the rich and giving to the poor using nothing more than his bow and arrow and sharp wit (along with his merry men, of course).

If I were to ask you what part "Loxley" plays in Robin's life, you would tell me that Loxley is his point of origin—his hometown. Now, because you know that Robin is from Loxley, you would look at Robin's behavior and be able to tell a little something about the place called Loxley. You might be fond of Loxley or dislike it depending upon how Robin interacts with you.

If you were poor, and Robin gave you stolen goods so that you could eat, you would say that Loxley produces some fine young men! If you were rich, and Robin stole from you to give to the poor, you would say that Loxley must be a foul place to produce such unethical individuals.

Neither one of these statements would be accurate. You cannot tell an entire town by a single individual, especially if that individual has made choices to depart from the straight and narrow.

What's more, if you asked me, "What is Loxley?" I wouldn't tell you that Loxley is Robin. Robin is simply *from* Loxley. Loxley is something bigger than Robin. Robin is merely a small part of Loxley and may not properly reflect Loxley depending upon the choices that he makes.

The word "of" means, "away" or "away from."[15] If something is of something else, it, like Robin of Loxley, is from that thing.

I tell you all about my childhood friend Robin to help frame this seemingly bold statement: fear is **not** a spirit.

Let that sink in.

Fear is not a spirit.

Now, there is a spirit of fear. God's Word is very clear about this. But **fear itself is not a spirit.**

———

> Now, there is a spirit of fear. God's Word is very
> clear about this. But *fear itself is not a spirit.*

---

15. "Of|Search Online Etymology Dictionary," Index, accessed November 29, 2018, https://www.etymonline.com/search?q=of.

Let's examine each word. Spirit. Of. Fear.

"Spirit" (*pnyoo'-mah* in the Greek) refers to persons that are not bound by bodies (i.e., the spirit of man (1 Thessalonians 5:23), Holy Spirit (John 20:22), deceiving spirits (1 Timothy 4:1)).

"Of" (as we've already seen) means "away, away from."

"Fear." The apostle Paul tells us in 2 Timothy 1 that there is a spirit that is of fear. This spirit of fear, as a part (not the whole) of fear, can no more give us a complete picture of fear than Robin could give us a complete picture of the town of Loxley. This is especially true when we consider that the spirit of fear very much strayed from what is right when he fell alongside Satan as a part of the one-third of angels who fell from heaven in the great rebellion.

What is more, you cannot argue that in knowing that there is a spirit of fear, that this means fear is a spirit. That is the same incorrect logic that would have us believe that Robin of Loxley tells us that Loxley is Robin. Fear is much larger than this spirit which 2 Timothy 1:7 refers to, so it requires more investigation.

I believe that the spirit of fear had a role to play in heaven that would give us a more complete view of fear, but because this spirit went astray, we can no longer trust its picture.

Fear is mentioned in the New King James Version of the Bible 354 times, but 2 Timothy 1:7 is the one and only place where the "spirit of fear" is mentioned. The Greek word used for "fear" in 2 Timothy 1:7 means "timidity, fearfulness, cowardice." It is the only time this Greek word is used in the New Testament.

It's interesting to me that the spirit of fear isn't a spirit of *phobeō* (derived from *phobos*). These two Greek words constitute the most common usage for the word "fear" in the New Testament. *Phobos* is the Greek word, as mentioned earlier, from which we derive the word *phobia*. There are many phobias out there. In researching phobias, I find that, arguably, you could have one phobia for every person, place, thing, or animal in life.[16]

Now, if the spirit of fear were a spirit of *phobos*, it would make a lot of sense to me since according to an article by the National Institute of Mental Health, 9.1% of the US population has had a specific (as opposed to general) phobia in the last year.[17] That constitutes approximately 29.7 million people— more than the entire population of the state of Texas.[18] Over twelve percent of the US population (40.9 million people— more than the entire population of California) have had a phobia at some time in their lives.[19]

You may agree with me in saying, "That's a lot of people," but those are just the diagnosed individuals! The general percentages of those who have a phobia are likely much higher. As an example, think of how many people have a fear of public speaking. Fear is prevalent, and it would make sense at first glance that there is an active, evil spirit of *phobos* behind it.

---

16. Amy Carmosino, "Facts About Phobias," Psych Central, October 8, 2018, accessed November 8, 2018, https://psychcentral.com/lib/facts-about-phobias.

17. "Specific Phobia," National Institute of Mental Health, November 2017, accessed November 8, 2018, https://www.nimh.nih.gov/health/statistics/specific-phobia.shtml.

18. Bureau, United States Census, 2017, accessed November 8 2018. https://www.census.gov/popclock.

19. Ibid

This just isn't the case, though. As we've discussed, we are told to fear (*phobos*) God (Acts 9:31). Because we are to *phobos* God, and we are told not to *phobos* other things, we are at an impasse if it is a spirit of *phobos*. Here's why: logically speaking, if the spirit of fear is a spirit of *phobos*, this spirit that directs us to fear the wrong things should also have the capacity to direct us toward fearing God since we are to *phobos* Him too. Of course, that's definitely not the case. The spirit of fear is evil, and, according to 2 Timothy 1:7, it positions itself against those things of God—power, love, and a sound mind.

So what is the spirit of fear if it is not a spirit of *phobos*?

In 2 Timothy 1, we see a young Timothy needing an injection of encouragement (as we all do from time to time). He receives this letter from his mentor, Paul, who begins the letter by reminding Timothy of who Paul is: "An apostle of Christ Jesus by the will of God, according to the promise of life in Christ Jesus" (v. 1 NASB). After establishing his own authority in Christ, Paul reminds Timothy of who the young man is: "my beloved son" (NASB). He goes on in verses 3–5 to encourage Timothy in various ways, and then in verse 6, he steps on the throttle.

Persecution and suffering were very real in Timothy and Paul's world, and Paul writes, "For this reason I remind you to kindle afresh the gift of God which is in you through the laying on of my hands" (v. 6). Why does Paul remind Timothy of this? As the preceding verses share with us, Timothy has sincere, genuine faith that is a part of a beautiful legacy, and it's a faith that warms Paul's heart. Paul's admonition and challenge, birthed out of love for Timothy, goes on to say:

> For God has not given us a spirit of fear, but of power and of
> love and of a sound mind. Therefore, do not be ashamed of the

testimony of our Lord, nor of me His prisoner, but share with me in the sufferings for the gospel according to the power of God (v. 7–8).

As I said, the chances of persecution and suffering were very real in Paul and Timothy's day. Being genuine in your faith had a real price, as it does many places in the world today. Is Paul telling Timothy not to have *phobos*? Actually, no.

Sometimes things that we must face seem very big, indeed. Those things can be very intimidating. They can make us shrink back. They can make us timid. The word timid bubbled up in the 1540s from the French word *timide* meaning, "easily frightened, shy."[20] Have you ever seen a shy child? I was one.

As a shy boy, I couldn't look an adult in the eye, much less carry on a conversation. There is an evil spirit that would seek to cause us to shrink back in a similar way. This spirit seeks to silence our voice and force us to look down, away from our opposition. This spirit is prevalent and hell-bent on relegating God's children to nothing more than quiet Bible readers who live well but speak seldom. The spirit of fear is not just interested in having us experience the emotion of fear; the spirit of fear wants for us to shrink back. This spirit will use the most penetrating lies, capitalize on *phobos*, and rejoice as we collapse into a nothing-heap of timidity.

The spirit of fear is not just interested in having us experience the emotion of fear;
the spirit of fear wants for us to shrink back.

---

20. "Timide | Search Online Etymology Dictionary," Index, accessed November 29, 2018, https://www.etymonline.com/search?q=timide.

When we listen to the sinister whispers of the spirit of fear, we risk seeing the thing that we have been convinced is bigger than us as bigger than God too.

Pastor Jimmy Evans says that the spirit of fear is a lying, prophetic spirit. This spirit tells us lies about what is to come with the purpose of getting us to shrink back and die. This should come as no surprise to us since our enemy comes to steal, kill, and destroy, and his language is lies (John 8:44; 10:10).

If you agree with the spirit of fear, you look at something and say, "That's bigger than me." Worse yet, you believe that the thing you fear is bigger than God. You wouldn't be the first to do this either.

> And they gave the children of Israel a bad report of the land which they had spied out, saying, "The land through which we have gone as spies is a land that devours its inhabitants, and all the people whom we saw in it are men of great stature. There we saw the giants (the descendants of Anak came from the giants); and we were like grasshoppers in our own sight, and so we were in their sight" (Numbers 13:32-33).

When the people of Israel decided not to go into the Promised Land, it wasn't just because they saw the Canaanites as bigger than them.

> Then the Lord said to Moses: "How long will these people reject Me? And how long will they not believe Me, with all the signs which I have performed among them?" (Numbers 14:11).

The people of Israel rejected God as God. They did not believe He was whom He said He was. They denied all that He did and saw mere men as bigger than God.

When we live our lives in a posture of timidity, shyness, and (honestly) cowardice, the ramifications on the world around us are devastating. If we are not the light to this world, the world will be left in darkness. If we are not the voice in the wilderness saying, "Make way for the Lord," this world will make way only for those things that are devastatingly destructive.

———

If we are not the light to this world,
the world will be left in darkness.

8

THE POSTURE OF FEAR

The spirit of fear has one ultimate goal: to force us into a *posture* of fear. *What does that look like?* you ask. The posture of fear is a posture carried first in one's heart. Like an inner compulsion that drives us to action, the posture of fear can be so forceful that we have no choice but to act on it. Let me explain.

——

The spirit of fear has one ultimate goal:
to force us into a *posture* of fear.

In Isaiah 6, Isaiah depicts his encounter with the Lord Almighty, high and exalted, seated on a throne. He tells us, in verse 1, that the train of His robe filled the temple. Majestic, mysterious creatures flew around calling out, "Holy, holy, holy is the Lord Almighty; the whole earth is full of His glory" (v. 3 NIV). I can only imagine that it was the most amazing sight Isaiah had ever seen! I'm confident that his words could not describe it and that our imaginations cannot recreate it.

What was Isaiah's reaction to beholding this glory? These words:

"Woe is me!... I am ruined! For I am a man of unclean lips, and I live among unclean people of unclean lips, and my eyes have seen the King, the Lord Almighty" (v. 5 NIV).

He fell. We don't know if Isaiah physically fell, but figuratively, he fell. At that moment, the reality of God's glory fell on him, and the weight of it was too much to bear. It caused him to cry out, as it would cause you or me, "Woe is me!"

In Ezekiel 1, we see Ezekiel's description of an "appearance of the likeness of the glory of the Lord." The prophet writes,

High above on the throne was a figure like that of a man. I saw that from what appeared to be his waist up he looked like glowing metal, as if full of fire, and that from there down he looked like fire; and brilliant light surrounded him. Like the appearance of a rainbow in the clouds on a rainy day, so was the radiance around him (v. 26–28 NIV).

It was absolutely breathtaking! Like Isaiah, Ezekiel was in awe. What was Ezekiel's reaction? "When I saw it, I fell facedown" (v. 28 NIV). He took the posture of fear. **The posture of fear is to fall down.**

John the apostle had a vision of Jesus. The moment he saw Jesus in His glory, John took the posture of fear.

When I turned to see who was speaking to me, I saw seven gold lampstands. And standing in the middle of the lampstands was someone like the Son of Man. He was wearing a long robe with a gold sash across his chest. His head and his hair were white like wool, as white as snow. And his eyes were like flames of fire. His feet were like polished bronze refined in a furnace, and his voice thundered like mighty ocean waves. He held seven stars in his right hand, and a sharp two-edged sword came from his mouth. And his face was like the sun in all its brilliance. When I saw him, I fell at his feet as if I were dead. But he laid his right hand on me and said, "Don't be afraid! I am the First and the Last. I am the living one. I died, but look—I am alive forever and ever! And I hold the keys of death and the grave (Revelation 1:12-18 NLT).

When we get a glimpse of who God is, we fall in fear. Our fear is based not on what He can do but in who He is. God has not given us a spirit of fear, but He does call us to a posture of fear.

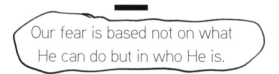

Our fear is based not on what He can do but in who He is.

Let's review what we know so far:

- Fear is neutral. It only becomes good or bad when it is attached to something good or bad.
- Fear is an emotion.
- There is a spirit of fear that seeks to make us shrink back and fall into the posture of fear.

Why does the posture of fear matter? For one, the posture of fear is the posture from which we often pray. When we fear the wrong things, we tend to pray from a place of fearing the wrong things rather than praying from a place of fear in God. These prayers tend to focus on the problem rather than the solution (God).

That's just the beginning, though. There is much more to discover as to why the posture of fear is important, but first, let's go ahead and answer that long-awaited question: **what is fear?**

9

FEAR DEFINED

Many people go through life thinking every step they take and every breath they breathe could be their last. Crippled by the fear of failure, the fear of rejection, or the fear of punishment, they move slowly and painfully through their days.

On the other end of the spectrum are those who seem to walk through life without a care in the world. Like a yin to the yang of the hyper-vigilant, they seem to glide through their years blissfully undisturbed. I will let you in on a secret, though: even these blessed souls experience fear. Fear touches *everyone*.

We've talked a good deal about fear, but now let's define it:

> Fear is the heightened sense of awareness to the dynamic of relationship between two beings/things, which recognizes the severe superiority of one over the other, and its control of the outcome of one's future.

████

Fear is the heightened sense of awareness to the dynamic of relationship between two beings/things, which recognizes the severe superiority of one over the other, and its control of the outcome of one's future.

Sound complicated? Let me explain. When we run across a poisonous snake on a path, we stop. Suddenly everything else in this world falls away. All that matters is the dynamic of relationship between us and the snake. Recognizing that the snake does, in fact, have the upper hand (quicker reflexes, sharp fangs, and paralyzing venom), we tread carefully, slowly, and desperately away. We hope to put as much distance as possible between the snake and us. That snake, so long as it is close, has severe superiority over us and has the potential to affect our future in a very tragic way.

Even someone who has had proper training and experience in handling snakes fears them. Their expressions of fear will probably differ from a person who lacks snake-handling training, but every move they make is passed through the heightened sense of awareness to the dynamic of their relationship to the snake. A snake charmer does not approach his snake in the same way he approaches his pet poodle. Why? Because he doesn't fear the dog; he fears the snake.

My dear friend and grandfather in the faith, Pastor Tommy Briggs, once said, "The thing you fear is what you focus on, and it will control you." When we fear something other than God, the focus of our hearts turns away from God and toward that thing. We then believe that this thing holds more power than God. We trust the words of fear more than the Word of God.

———

We trust the words of fear more than the Word of God.

When we truly fear God, the fear of everything else falls away. When we fear Him properly, we take account of how our current position, decision, thought, circumstance, or step affects our relationship with Him. And we see that our relation to Him is very, very close, because He is a good Father, and nothing can separate us from His love (Romans 8:35–38).

In *Freedom From Fear,* Neil Anderson and Rich Miller write, "We are recognizing Him [God] as the only legitimate fear object when we submit to Him."[21] We will all submit to something in this life. Are you submitted to God?

God made us to walk through this life in need of an anchor. Even if we tell ourselves that we are walking through this life anchored to nothing, we are anchored to something. The thing we fear will always be our anchor.

It just might be that we were made to fear God, the very source of the anchor of our souls (Hebrews 6:19).

———

It just might be that we were made to fear God, the very source of the anchor of our souls

We were made to walk through this life asking, "How is this decision affecting the dynamic of the relationship between God and me?" Living this way allows us to answer this question honestly: *Do I fear God?*

In *Addicted to Busy,* Pastor Brady Boyd quotes Martyn Lloyd-Jones' powerful prayer, which personifies this posture of God-focus:

Throughout the whole of this day, everything I do, and say, and attempt, and think, and imagine, is going to be done under the eye

21. Neil T. Anderson and Rich Miller, *Freedom From Fear.* (Eugene, OR: Harvest House Publishers, 1999.)

*of God. He is going to be with me; He sees everything; He knows
everything. There is nothing I can do or attempt but God is fully
aware of it all.*[22]

When was the last time you included God in your decision
making? When was the last time you asked God whom you
should be doing life with? Do you fear God?

Hear this: fearing God is **not** fearing that we will lose
our salvation if we have a misstep. Jesus said no one can
take us from His hand (John 10:28), and nothing can
separate us from His love (Romans 8:38–39). Once we are
saved, we are seated in the heavenly places (Ephesians
2:6), and there are no evictions for saved-by-grace-
through-faith individuals.

I fear God in much the same way that I fear my wife. All
that I do is passed through the filter of "How will this affect
the dynamic of my relationship with my wife?" I don't make
large purchases without talking to my wife first because that
would affect her, and thus affect our relationship. I don't cheat
on my wife because that would adversely affect our relationship. My consideration of my wife is what Paul refers to in 1
Corinthians 7:33 when he says, "But he who is married cares
about the things of the world—how he may please *his* wife."
Being married gives me the responsibility of considering the
dynamic between myself and God *and* myself and my wife.

Here's the amazing thing: both are motivated by love. I
don't remain faithful to God and faithful to my wife out of fear
of punishment. I remain faithful out of love. I consider closely

---

22. Brady Boyd, *Addicted to Busy.* (Colorado Springs: David C Cook
    Publishing Company, 2014.)

the relationship between myself and God and between myself and my wife because I love them both. Fear has to do with relationship.

———

I don't remain faithful to God and faithful to my wife out of fear of punishment. I remain faithful out of love.

Those who follow the right path fear the Lord;
    those who take the wrong path despise him
(Proverbs 14:2 NLT).

This is how "perfect love casts out fear" *and* "the fear of God" can coexist.

There is no fear in love; but perfect love casts out fear, because fear involves torment. But he who fears has not been made perfect in love (1 John 4:18).

Let's not miss this: "fear involves torment." Other translations say, "Fear involves punishment" (NASB, NLT). Here is the context of the verse:

Love has been perfected among us in this: that we may have boldness in the day of judgment; because as He is, so are we in this world. There is no fear in love; but perfect love casts out fear, because fear involves torment. But he who fears has not been made perfect in love. We love Him because He first loved us (1 John 4:17–19).

John urges us to have boldness in the day of judgment, not fearing punishment or torment. Those who do fear punishment have not been perfected in love—they haven't received God's love. God's love is the only perfect love there is.

———

God's love is the only perfect love there is.

Though it has been used this way by many well-meaning teachers, this verse does not invite us to live a life devoid of fear. We must fear God. We must not, however, fear punishment. We are invited to live a life devoid of the fear of punishment.

Going back to Acts 5, we see Ananias and Sapphira meeting death when they lied to the Holy Spirit about how much money they had gotten for their land. Verses five and eleven tell us that their death brought, "great fear upon all the church." Deciphering this verse to know whether the people feared God or feared His punishment is difficult.

If fearing God's punishment separates us from Him (we'll unpack this in the next section) and fearing Him causes us to draw close to God, we can look to Acts 9 for an answer:

> The church then had peace throughout Judea, Galilee, and Samaria, and it became stronger as the believers lived in the fear of the Lord. And with the encouragement of the Holy Spirit, it also grew in numbers (NLT)

A tree can be identified by its fruit. The fruit expressed in Acts 9 from fearing the Lord was peace, strength, encouragement, and growth. The church depicted in Acts feared God well. Fearing the punishment of God does not bear the fruit that God desires for our lives. No peace comes when we walk through life afraid that He will strike us.

The people of Israel stood between the Egyptian army and an unpassable sea. In their moment of desperation, God split the sea, they walked through, and the sea came crashing down on their enemies! The Israelites had just seen God's deliverance through the plagues, and this act was one more display of the lengths He was willing to go to for their freedom. He is so good!

In Exodus 14:31 we read, "Thus Israel saw the great work which the Lord had done in Egypt; so the people feared the Lord, and believed the Lord and His servant Moses." God's miraculous power and might brought them to fear the Lord. Or did it?

Later in Exodus 20, the people of Israel arrive at the place where God wants to meet with them: Mount Sinai. God tells Moses that His people are not to come up, and they don't take much convincing.

> Now all the people witnessed the thunderings, the lightning flashes, the sound of the trumpet, and the mountain smoking; and when the people saw it, they trembled and stood afar off. Then they said to Moses, "You speak with us, and we will hear; but let not God speak with us, lest we die (Exodus 20:18-19).

They witnessed yet more of God's greatness, and they trembled!

Moses' reaction speaks on the duality of fear:

> And Moses said to the people, "Do not fear; for God has come to test you, and that His fear may be before you, so that you may

not sin." So the people stood afar off, but Moses drew near the thick darkness where God was (Exodus 20:20–21).

Moses says, "Do not fear" but then says to fear God! What does he mean? He means they should not fear God's punishment, but that they should fear *Him*. So long as they accepted God's path to relationship with Him (through their deliverer Moses), they didn't need to fear God's punishment. They need only fear Him.

The same is true for us today. So long as we accept God's path to relationship with Him (through our deliverer Jesus), we do not need to fear God's punishment. His perfect love, displayed through Jesus, cast that out. We only need to fear Him.

———

So long as we accept God's path to relationship
with Him (through our deliverer Jesus),
we do not need to fear God's punishment.

If we could manage to fear God properly, life might look a little different for all of us. How do we do that? Well, the writer of Psalm 34 implies to us that it must be learned:

Come, you children, listen to me;
I will teach you the fear of the Lord (v. 11)

How do you learn to fear the Lord? The short answer is through reading God's Word. In Philippians 4:6–9, the apostle Paul writes,

Be anxious for nothing, but in everything by prayer and supplication, with thanksgiving, let your requests be made known to

God; and the peace of God, which surpasses all understanding, will guard your hearts and minds through Christ Jesus. Finally, brethren, whatever is true, whatever is honorable, whatever is right, whatever is pure, whatever is lovely, whatever is of good repute, if there is any excellence and if anything worthy of praise, dwell on these things. The things you have learned and received and heard and seen in me, practice these things, and the God of peace will be with you.

Think about what you are doing when you obey this verse: when something comes along that is trying to make you anxious (worry), you turn your attention to God, make Him the source of truth and comfort, and He gives you the peace needed to guard your heart. This is the act of fearing Him. When something else tries to steal your fear, you turn your fear to God instead!

When something else tries to steal your fear, you turn your fear to God instead.

10

———

FIRST FEAR

The principle of *first mention* is important. The first time we see something in Scripture, whether it be a word, a concept, or an event, it serves as a benchmark for us to return to for clarity and definition throughout the rest of Scripture.

The first time fear is mentioned in Scripture is Genesis 3:10:

> He said, "I heard the sound of You in the garden, and I was afraid because I was naked; so I hid myself."

Here we see Adam and Eve eating the forbidden fruit. It's an amazing story worth your time to read again. God comes to Adam and Eve and asks, "What have you done?" Their answer is not to confess what they did but to say whose fault it was. There's a lot we could unpack here, but what I want to know is, "What exactly did they fear?"

I believe they feared punishment. According to Dr. Henry Cloud, punishment is payment for wrongdoing. Punishment looks back at past wrongs and looks for payment.[23] Imagine yourself in their shoes! They suspected that God would come and punish them, but they had no idea how. What would they

———

23. Cloud and Townsend, *Boundaries.*

have to pay? Maybe He would crush them? Maybe He would reject them? Who knows? They had never disobeyed God before this moment.

It's interesting to me what their reaction was to this fear of punishment: they hid themselves. They didn't hide what they *did*—they hid *themselves*! When we walk through this life fearing punishment, we don't hide the things we do (though sometimes we try), we hide who we are! What's worse, you cannot hide what you did without hiding who you are. The more we embrace God's grace, the more we are able to be ourselves because we are no longer trying to hide the things we have done.

When we hide as a reaction to the fear of punishment, we will spend our entire lives robbing ourselves and the world of who God made us to be! When we fear God, it brings out the best in us; when we fear His punishment, we disappear and separate ourselves from Him. The fear of God's punishment separates us from Him; the fear of God Himself draws us closer to Him.

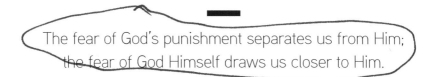

The fear of God's punishment separates us from Him; the fear of God Himself draws us closer to Him.

Nothing makes you more alive than fearing God, and that's why Jesus came—for life more abundant (John 10:10).

God said in Genesis 2:16–17 that if Adam and Eve ate of the tree of the knowledge of good and evil (which they did), they would die. God never said that He would be the one to kill them. He just said that they would die. But they hid from Him. They hid out of fear of His punishment.

Until they sinned, the fear Adam and Eve had for God was a thing of unparalleled beauty. I imagine they walked through the garden keenly aware and focused on how their actions affected their relationship with God. Adam and Eve were made by God Himself. Genesis 3:8 tells us that God was walking in the garden in the cool of the day. It wouldn't be a stretch to say that this may have been His habit. Every step they took, every breath they breathed (which God first breathed into them), and every turn they made was passed through a heightened sense of awareness of the dynamic of their relationship with God. I'm sure it was a beautiful thing to behold. This was their reality—their posture—right until the moment they ate the forbidden fruit. The moment they decided to listen to the enemy, they decided to fear something other than God; they decided to fear missing out.

The enemy said in Genesis 3:4, "You will not surely die. For God knows that in the day you eat of it your eyes will be opened, and you will be like God, knowing good and evil." In this moment the enemy told them that God was holding out on them.

When we open the door to fearing things other than God, it is a slippery, downward slope. First, Adam and Eve feared missing out. Then they feared punishment. Separated from the presence of God, they found themselves spiritually dead.

Fear: Opposite of Faith?

Before we move onto our next section, I want to visit one last question: *is fear the opposite of faith?* In my personal church history, fear has often been pitted against faith as the opposite, incorrect reaction to a situation that seems too big for us. Now knowing the definition of fear, this idea seems to crumble.

I've heard it said, "Faith is listening to God while fear is listening to the devil." If this were true, then the devil would actually be the main catalyst to steering us toward fearing God. If listening to the enemy equated to fear, then he would be our biggest cheerleader in fearing God. The devil would be crying out, "All you Christ-followers! Fear God!" But, as we well know, he doesn't. Fear isn't as simple as listening to the enemy. Let's revisit the story of Abraham:

> "Don't lay a hand on the boy!" the angel said. "Do not hurt him in any way, for now I know that you truly fear God. You have not withheld from me even your son, your only son" (Genesis 22:12).

This is a powerful moment in the story of Abraham. This father had gone up the mountain with his son Isaac with the full and total intent of sacrificing him. He was not faking it or hesitating. In fact, in Hebrews 11:17–19 we see,

> By faith Abraham, when he was tested, offered up Isaac, and he who had received the promises offered up his only begotten son, of whom it was said, "In Isaac your seed shall be called," concluding that God was able to raise him up, even from the dead, from which he also received him in a figurative sense.

I love that! What amazing trust! Abraham was willing to sacrifice Isaac because he believed that "God was able to raise him up, even from the dead."

There is something to note here in Abraham's story. Before the knife was even raised in the air, Abraham had faith. As we discussed, faith comes by *hearing*. Each time that Abraham heard, he put faith in what God was saying. However, it wasn't until Abraham went all in, no-holds-barred, to sacrifice Isaac that we see these words: "now I know that you truly fear God."

Faith doesn't oppose fear; faith precedes it. You have to have faith before you get to fear. I will never fear the snake unless someone tells me that it might be a good idea for my health to fear the snake. If I don't hear them say that or I don't put my faith in what they say, I will never arrive at that place of fear in my heart.

———

Faith doesn't oppose fear; faith precedes it.

First, we must hear. Then we may have faith. Then we can fear. When that fear is placed in God because we hear who He says He is, and we put our faith in that, then we can enjoy all that fearing God promises.

Now let's talk about worship.

11

WORSHIP

Then Abraham lifted his eyes and looked, and there behind him was a ram caught in a thicket by its horns. So Abraham went and took the ram, and offered it up for a burnt offering instead of his son

—Genesis 22:13

Have you ever wondered where fear came from? Sure, there is a spirit of fear, and this spirit will come to us and try to get us to fear all of the wrong things. This spirit will tell us lies and convince us that things other than God have control over our future. We've established this much. But, as we've also established, fear constitutes a larger picture than just this spirit. So where did fear come from?

When I was a little boy in children's classes at church, the answer to every question was "Jesus." Well, at least 95% of the time. "Jesus" became my default answer. The teacher would ask, "Who is the only perfect person who ever lived?" I would confidently answer, "Jesus!" Correct. The teacher would ask, "How do you make it through a tough day?" I would put my shoulders back, my chin up, and answer, "Jesus!" Correct. "Where did fear come from?" Again, with all of my might, I would answer, "Jesus!" *Wrong.* My teacher would reply, "No, fear came from Satan."

Like many other believers, I was raised to believe that our enemy created fear. "Fear is of the devil" was the general understanding.

But did it? Allow me to revisit the question we were challenged with earlier: did Satan create fear?

Let's take a moment to look at all that Satan has created. If you turn your Bible to... well ... if you think about ... Okay. I can't find anything.

Of course not! Satan is a creature. He was *created*; he is not the Creator. In fact, he has created **nothing**.

There are some things that the enemy would like to convince us that he's created—things such as pleasure, fun, sex, and even fear. But this just isn't the case. Satan can't create anything. He can only pervert things. Our enemy tries to pervert everything God has created. That's what liars do. They don't create truth; they twist it.

Satan didn't create fear. God did. Let's read what Colossians 1:16 says about Jesus again:

> For by Him all things were created that are in heaven and that are on earth, visible and invisible, whether thrones or dominions or principalities or powers. All things were created through Him and for Him.

Why in the world would God create something like fear? We often ask questions like this. (Personally, I want to know why God created wasps!) We look at things on this earth that we don't understand (usually things we deem negative) and then allow the enemy to use them to chip away at the character of God. We allow him to use things like pain, brokenness, loss, fear, and even wasps to question God's goodness, faithfulness, care, and love.

I'm not going to attempt to shift your perspective on all of the hurt or difficulty in this world, but let's talk about wasps. I *hate* them. They have stung me, my dog, and my friends. They come by, looking sleek and evil, and threaten my perfectly good day. Sometimes they even come in my house. Oh boy, that's never a good situation for my wife! She takes hating wasps to a whole other level, and she is terrified of them.

Did God create wasps? Yes. Why? What good could there be in wasps?

While they do sting from time to time, wasps serve a great purpose in pollinating plants, eating other insects (keeping the population down), feeding their young with caterpillar and leaf beetle larvae (major threats to plants and crops), and more![24] Without wasps, we would be living with piles of dead bugs (they eat dead bugs too), our crops would be damaged, and we wouldn't have as many pretty flowers! It kind of changes your perspective on wasps, doesn't it? They actually do have a purpose.

Fear was created by God for a purpose too:

I know that whatever God does,
It shall be forever.
Nothing can be added to it,
And nothing taken from it.
God does it, that men should fear before Him
(Ecclesiastes 3:14).

In *Lead Like Jesus,* Ken Blanchard and Phil Hodges share:

---

24. Debbie Hadley, "What Good Are Wasps?" ThoughtCo, January 24, 2019, accessed April 11, 2019, https://www.thoughtco.com/what-good-are -wasps-1968081.

The capacity to fear is a gift from God. When applied as intended, fear can keep us focused on doing the right thing for the right reasons. Yet what we actually do with the gift of our capacity to fear often prevents us from enjoying its benefits. Instead of enhancing life as a dimension of keeping our focus on God, fear has poisoned human relationships ever since man stepped out of God's will.[25]

Imagine that you are Abraham, and in an amazingly reckless act of obedience, you go to sacrifice the thing that means the most to you. You don't attempt to sacrifice it out of religion, (because it's the thing that you are "supposed" to do), but because the living God told you to. As you draw the knife, and by doing so choose to lay down your dream of being "successful," God steps in and says, "Wait."

In the following moments, God recognizes that you are not just a person who puts faith in what He says, but you are also a person who fears Him. How amazing would it have been to be recognized by God in this powerful way?

What was the difference between faith and fear for Abraham? Faith was enough to have him obey God, but fear was proven *when* he obeyed. <u>You obey what you fear</u>.

Faith was enough to have him obey God,
but fear was proven *when* he obeyed.

By faith Abraham, when he was tested, offered up Isaac, and he who had received the promises offered up his only begotten son, of whom it was said, "In Isaac your seed shall be

---

25. Ken Blanchard, Phil Hodges, and Phyllis Hendry, *Lead Like Jesus* (Nashville: Thomas Nelson, 2016).

called," concluding that God *was* able to raise *him* up, even from the dead, from which he also received him in a figurative sense (Hebrews 11:17–19).

Had Abraham feared never having a son, not having the promise fulfilled, or being disappointed by God, he never would have gone as far as he did with sacrificing Isaac. It was like God was saying, "I know all that you have the opportunity to fear, but I see that you fear Me." It's a powerful moment!

Put yourself back in the story: as you realize that your son— your future, your promise, and your dream—will actually be with you at dinner tonight and breakfast tomorrow, you look up, and you see something else of value: a ram. Rams can provide food, clothing, and more sheep, and they can also be sacrificed. They can be used for worship, and that's what Abraham did.

Why did God create fear? Because fear leads to worship. Deuteronomy 6:13 shows us the connection: "You shall fear only the Lord your God; and you shall worship Him and swear by His name."

___

Why did God create fear?
Because fear leads to worship.

Jesus did many miracles. When we read about them, we often see people's reactions as a connection between fear and worship:

They were all struck with astonishment and began glorifying God; and they were filled with fear, saying, "We have seen remarkable things today" (Luke 5:26).

Fear gripped them all, and they began glorifying God, saying, "A great prophet has arisen among us!" and, "God has visited His people!" (Luke 7:16).

Now when the multitudes saw it, they marveled [feared] and glorified God, who had given such power to men (Matthew 9:8). We also see this connection in the Old Testament:

"The covenant that I have made with you, you shall not forget, nor shall you fear other gods. But the Lord your God you shall fear; and He will deliver you from the hand of all your enemies." However, they did not listen, but they did according to their earlier custom. So while these nations feared the Lord, they also served their idols; their children likewise and their grandchildren, as their fathers did, so they do to this day (2 Kings 17:38-41),

If you fear the Lord and serve Him and obey His voice, and do not rebel against the commandment of the Lord, then both you and the king who reigns over you will continue following the Lord your God (1 Samuel 12:14).

Only fear the Lord, and serve Him in truth with all your heart; for consider what great things He has done for you (1 Samuel 12:24).

Worship the LORD with reverence [fear] And rejoice with trembling (Psalm 2:11).

For the Lord is great and greatly to be praised;
He is to be feared above all gods (Psalm 96:4).

I'll say it again: Fear leads to worship. **What you fear, you worship**. "Worship is an act of reverence and has the root idea of trembling or fear—being in awe of God."[26] There is a key component that relates worship and fear.

———

What you fear, you worship.

Let's look again at a few of the verses that we covered earlier:

> In the year that King Uzziah died, I saw the Lord sitting on a throne, high and lifted up, and the train of His robe filled the temple. Above it stood seraphim; each one had six wings: with two he covered his face, with two he covered his feet, and with two he flew. And one cried to another and said:
>
> "Holy, holy, holy is the Lord of hosts;
> The whole earth is full of His glory!"
> And the posts of the door were shaken by the voice of him who cried out, and the house
> was filled with smoke.
> So I said:
> "Woe is me, for I am undone!
> Because I am a man of unclean lips,
> And I dwell in the midst of a people of unclean lips;
> For my eyes have seen the King,
> The Lord of hosts" (Isaiah 6:1–5).

> "High above on the throne was a figure like that of a man. I saw that from what appeared to be his waist up he looked like glowing metal, as if full of fire, and that from there down he looked like fire; and brilliant light surrounded him. Like the

---

26. Blanchard, Hodges, and Hendry, *Lead Like Jesus.*

appearance of a rainbow in the clouds on a rainy day, so was the radiance around him" (Ezekiel 1:24-28).

"When I turned to see who was speaking to me, I saw seven gold lampstands. And standing in the middle of the lampstands was someone like the Son of Man. He was wearing a long robe with a gold sash across his chest. His head and his hair were white like wool, as white as snow. And his eyes were like flames of fire. His feet were like polished bronze refined in a furnace, and his voice thundered like mighty ocean waves. He held seven stars in his right hand, and a sharp two-edged sword came from his mouth. And his face was like the sun in all its brilliance. When I saw him, I fell at his feet as if I were dead. But he laid his right hand on me and said, "Don't be afraid! I am the First and the Last. I am the living one. I died, but look—I am alive forever and ever! And I hold the keys of death and the grave" (Revelation 1:12-18).

As mere humans come face to face with the living God, holy fear forces them into a posture. This posture is the posture of fear. **The posture of fear is worship.**

When Jesus healed the paralytic and forgave his sins, we read,

Now when the multitudes saw it, they marveled [feared] and glorified [esteem as glorious; from praise] God, who had given such power to men (Matthew 9:8).

You worship what you fear. While this may be a new revelation to you and me, it isn't to the angels in heaven. Look at them when they come into contact with people:

And an angel of the Lord suddenly stood before them, and the glory of the Lord shone around them; and they were terribly frightened. But the angel said to them, "Do not be afraid; for behold, I bring you good news of great joy which will be for all the people" (Luke 2:9-10).

We have read this verse many, many times. The angel shows up before the shepherds to tell them of the Messiah's coming! It's awesome! But what if the angel is saying something far more profound than what we have read in the past?

The angel tells them, "Do not be afraid; for behold, I bring you good news." In the past, I have read this as, "Don't worry. I'm bringing good news, not bad news." What if it's more than that, though? What if the angel is saying, "I'm bringing good news, but I'm just the messenger. So don't fear me. Fear God"? In Luke 2, the word for "angel of the Lord" is "messenger."

Why would an angel (messenger of the Lord) not want to be feared? Because that angel is *from* the Lord; he is not the Lord. That angel knows that what we fear, we worship. That angel knows that only God is to be worshipped.

John is face to face with an angel of the Lord in Revelation:

Then he said to me, "Write, 'Blessed are those who are invited to the marriage supper of the Lamb.'" And he said to me, "These are true words of God." Then I fell at his feet to worship him. But he said to me, "Do not do that; I am a fellow servant of yours and your brethren who hold the testimony of Jesus; worship God. For the testimony of Jesus is the spirit of prophecy" (Revelation 19:9–10).

I, John, am the one who heard and saw these things. And when I heard and saw, I fell down to worship at the feet of the angel who showed me these things. But he said to me, "Do not do that. I am a fellow servant of yours and of your brethren the prophets and of those who heed the words of this book. Worship God" (Revelation 22:8–9)

Angels of the Lord know that God alone is to be worshipped, so God alone is to be feared. Unfortunately, the sad reality is that not all angels are of the Lord. One third fell from heaven with the enemy (Revelation 12:4,9). *We have an enemy who wants to be worshipped.*

In Matthew 3, Jesus goes to the Jordan River, and His cousin John baptizes Him. The Holy Spirit arrives on the scene, and God the Father pronounces that Jesus is His "beloved Son, in whom I'm well pleased" (Matthew 3:15).

In the very next chapter, Jesus is tempted in the wilderness.

> And he [Satan] said to Him [Jesus], "All these things I will give You if You will fall down and worship me" (Matthew 4:9).

Satan wants to be worshipped! He wants to be worshipped by God Himself and by anyone who looks like God (i.e., us). We were created in God's image (Genesis 1:27), and if Satan can get us to worship him, it's the next best thing to God Himself worshipping him.

It's interesting to me that the enemy wants nothing more than to be worshipped, and we so often find ourselves in fear of him and what he can do. It's almost as if our enemy knows that if he can get us to fear him, we will worship him.

Pastor Robert Morris says, "As much as you want to be devoted to God, fear will slowly and surely steal your devotion to God... What you fear the most is what you will be devoted to the most."[27]

---

27. Robert Morris. "The Thief of Devotion". Gateway Church, Southlake, Texas, May 27, 2006.

Satan knows that if he can get us to fear him, he will be able to steal our devotion and eventually our worship. In Scripture, our enemy is referred to as a serpent (Genesis 3:1). Serpents slither, sneak, and creep in unnoticed.

Some of us have been worshipping the enemy without even knowing it. When you fear the wrong thing, you worship the wrong thing. If you fear rejection, you will slowly but surely find yourself worshipping acceptance. If you fear death, you will slowly but surely find yourself worshipping "living." If you fear failure, you will worship success. If you fear not having enough, you will worship your work. The enemy will use this to slither, sneak, and creep unnoticed into your life, and he will steal, kill, and destroy you in ways you never saw coming.

> When you fear the wrong thing, you worship the wrong thing.

Know this: if you are worshipping success, you are not worshipping God in that area of your life. If you are worshipping acceptance, you are not worshipping God in that area of your life. If you are worshipping anything else, you cannot also be worshipping God. How do I know?

> No one can serve two masters; for either he will hate the one and love the other, or else he will be loyal to the one and despise the other. You cannot serve God and mammon (Matthew 6:2).

Matt Papa suggests in his book *Look and Live* that idols cannot be removed; they can only be replaced. You can wish all you want not to worship success, but it's impossible to remove success from the idol of your heart. You can only replace success with God.[28] In the same way, you cannot just "not fear." You have to fear something just as you have to worship something. Just as something will always be sitting on the altar of your heart, you will always be in awe of that thing. You will always fear something. You will always look to something or someone before you make a decision, walk a path, think a thought, or speak a word.

Do you remember Peter's short-lived attempt to walk on water?

> Now in the fourth watch of the night Jesus went to them, walking on the sea. And when the disciples saw Him walking on the sea, they were troubled, saying, "It is a ghost!" And they cried out for fear.
>
> But immediately Jesus spoke to them, saying, "Be of good cheer! It is I; do not be afraid."
>
> And Peter answered Him and said, "Lord, if it is You, command me to come to You on the water."
>
> So He said, "Come." And when Peter had come down out of the boat, he walked on the water to go to Jesus. But when he saw that the wind was boisterous, he was afraid; and beginning to sink he cried out, saying, "Lord, save me!"
>
> And immediately Jesus stretched out His hand and caught him, and said to him, "O you of little faith, why did you doubt?" And when they got into the boat, the wind ceased.

---

28. Matt Papa (2014). *Look and Live.* Baker Publishing Group.

Then those who were in the boat came and worshiped Him, saying, "Truly You are the Son of God" (Matthew 14:25–33).

The object of Peter's fear started with a fear of death and destruction by way of the storm, shifted to a fear of a thought-to-be ghost, and finally to Jesus. When the focus of his fear shifted to Jesus, he walked on water. When the focus of his fear shifted back to the storm, he sank. Peter began to sink because he feared the storm more than he feared Jesus; he was more concerned with his relationship to the storm than his relationship to Jesus. He elevated the storm's ability to affect his future above Jesus' ability to affect his future. He could not fear both at the same time.

Look at Jesus in the Garden of Gethsemane. Can you imagine the opportunity for fear that Jesus had while knowing the pain and torture that lay ahead? He asked for it to be taken away three times (Matthew 26:36–44). Matthew 26:38 says Jesus was "exceedingly sorrowful," and Mark 14:33 says He was "troubled and deeply distressed." He was not looking forward to what God the Father was asking Him to do.

We know that Jesus responded, "Not my will, but Your will," but how could He make this statement in the face of such dreaded darkness?

Hebrews 5:7 tells us,

[Jesus] who, in the days of His flesh, when He had offered up prayers and supplications, with vehement cries and tears to Him who was able to save Him from death, and was heard because of His godly fear.

Isaiah 11:2, speaking prophetically of Jesus, tells us,

The Spirit of the Lord will rest on Him, The spirit of wisdom and understanding, The spirit of counsel and strength, The spirit of knowledge and the fear of the Lord.

Jesus feared God the Father! He feared the Father more than the pain, more than the tormentors, and more than the rejection. He didn't fear death enough to worship temporary life. He feared His Father enough to take the cup of suffering for all of humanity. He feared God above all else, so how could He fear anything else?

Remember that we discussed Pharaoh's people throwing the Israelite's babies into the Nile because they feared the Pharaoh? We asked the difficult question, "How many threw their own babies into the Nile?" Even if they didn't, by giving over their babies, they may as well have thrown them in themselves. When the people threw the babies into the river, they sacrificed them to the god of the Nile. The Egyptians believed that Hapi was associated with the nutrients and fertility provided by the Nile River. They believed him to be the provider of fertility. The Israelites' fear of Pharaoh drove them to worship something other than God.

God alone will be worshipped. One day, every knee will bow before Him (Romans 14:11). The enemy has no choice but to worship God when he is confronted by Him. In Mark 5 we see the demoniac confronted by Jesus.

Seeing Jesus from a distance, he ran up and bowed down before Him; and shouting with a loud voice, he said, "What business do we have with each other, Jesus, Son of the Most High God? I implore You by God, do not torment me!" (Mark 5:6–7).

The enemy feared God, so he worshipped Jesus.

One day, when we are all face to face with Him, we will fall in fear. All will worship.

> When I saw Him, I fell at His feet like a dead man. And He placed His right hand on me, saying, "Do not be afraid; I am the first and the last, and the living One; and I was dead, and behold, I am alive forevermore, and I have the keys of death and of Hades" (Revelation 1:17-18).

God did not give us a spirit of fear, but He did give us a posture of fear. "All of life becomes a worship experience if you are always aware of God's presence and do everything to His glory."[29] Said another way, when you walk in fear, you are walking in worship.

———

God did not give us a spirit of fear,
but He did give us a posture of fear.

God gave us fear so that we could worship Him, but why? It might just have something to do with our freedom.

---

29. Blanchard, Hodges, and Hendry, *Lead Like Jesus*.

12

FREEDOM

"Let my people go, that they may serve Me."

—Exodus 8:1

I was afraid of people. I was afraid of marriage. I was afraid of conflict, the future, and failure. I was afraid of amounting to nothing. I was afraid of things that I didn't know I was afraid of. Fear of all the wrong things ruled me on so many levels.

I remember once standing toe to toe with a very well-meaning senior on my high school soccer team. He asked me if he could have another cupcake. In a moment of sweaty nervousness, I froze. To give him another cupcake was to rob myself of the opportunity to have one, but to tell him that this last one was for me was to risk rejection! I didn't eat a cupcake that day. The sad part was that the cupcakes were made by my mom for me (and the team). The sadder part was that this wasn't the only time that this happened. I let people walk all over me on a regular basis.

Moses had some fears, but he stood toe to toe with Pharaoh. "Let my people go!" he called out on behalf of God. We know how the story ends: God frees His people from Egypt. He frees His people from slavery and bondage.

We can now assert that Moses moved forward with what he did because he feared God above all else, but why did God send him on such a scary mission in the first place? Was it just to make Moses uncomfortable? Was it to test him? Maybe some of both of those options, but what does Scripture say?

The short answer is that God wanted to set His people free. But why? Why would He want to set His people free?

Exodus 5:1, 7:16, 8:1, 8:20, 9:1, 9:13, and 10:3 give us the answer: to worship Him! God wants us to be set free to worship Him!

———

God wants us to be set free to worship Him!

As we discussed, if the Israelites killed their own babies, they were doing so out of a fear of Pharaoh and potentially because of a worship of the local gods. God had to take them through a process of turning them to fear Him, because if you don't fear God, you will not worship Him.

According to Pastor Robert Morris, worship is love expressed.[30] When we are free, we are able to love the Lord our God wholly—heart, soul, mind, and strength—just as we are commanded:

> "And you shall love the Lord your God with all your heart, with all your soul, with all your mind, and with all your strength" (Mark 12:30).

---

30. Robert Morris. "What Is Church?" Gateway Church, Southlake, Texas, January 12, 2013.

Pastor Jimmy Evans explains that bondage is anything that serves as an impediment to loving God or others in any one of these areas (heart, soul, mind, or strength).[31] We are commanded to love God this way and to love others (Mark 12:31).

You can be sure that while the Israelites were captive in Egypt, it affected the way they loved God and loved each other. They needed to be free, and they needed to worship.

Have you ever asked, "Why do we need to worship?" Certainly, God is worthy of worship. He alone is to be worshipped (Exodus 20:3, Luke 4:8), but, if I may be so human and bold, how does that affect us? What's in it for us?

Now, before you get offended, I want you to know that I ask that question with all humility and with the realization that there is no better thing for us as humans than to serve God. There is no better payoff! Life eternal and life abundant are pretty stellar by-products of submitting to Him, so what's the payoff of worshipping Him?

Over the years I've been to various nights of worship. People from the church and outside the church would gather to worship God.

One of these worship nights, I noticed that there were two types of people attending. One type was there to worship God. They came hungry and ready to meet with Him. It was a beautiful thing!

Others missed the purpose of the night. This second group of people seemed to be there to worship the person leading instead of the God that this worship leader was trying to lead them to. They were there to worship the created instead of the

---

31. "Freedom Meeting." Jimmy Evans. May 15, 2018.

Creator. It may seem to be difficult to tell the difference, but in that moment it was obvious.

As I looked around, I noticed that there were people peppered throughout the congregation who wore clothes like the leader and even did their hair like the leader. I wouldn't be surprised if these worship-leader-worshippers even talked like the leader!

Why was this? It's simple: you become what you worship. These people weren't themselves. They were lost. They were becoming something that they weren't: an empty copy of one who had actual life.

You become what you worship.

Psalm 115 tells us about those who make and worship idols. An idol is anything other than God that we allow to take the places in our lives and hearts that only God should have. Verse 8 says,

> Those who make them are like them;
> So is everyone who trusts in them.

What you worship, you become! This statement alone is worth enough time to ask God, "What do I worship?" But here's why this is important: what you worship you *become*! Becoming is a process of change. What you worship changes you!

Becoming is a process of change.
What you worship changes you!

And do not be conformed to this world, but be transformed by the renewing of your mind, that you may prove what is that good and acceptable and perfect will of God (Romans 12:2).

Being "conformed" and "transformed" are processes of change. You are changing every day! As you live life, as you worship, you will be changed into the image of this world, or you will be changed more and more into the image of God. The question becomes, *what are you worshipping?* What you worship will change you—for better or worse!

What you hear, you put faith in. What you put faith in determines what you fear, what you fear determines what you worship, and what you worship determines what you become. You only have two choices—you will become free, or you will become bound—and all of that stems from what you stop to hear.

God wants us to worship Him because when we do, we look more and more like Him. We are able to love like Him, think like Him, and be holy like He is holy. The more like Him we become, the more ourselves we become because we are made in His image.

What do you fear? If it isn't God, it will lead to bondage and death. How do I know? Habakkuk 2:18–19 tells us about idols:

> What good is an idol carved by man, or a cast image that deceives you? How foolish to trust in your own creation—a god that can't even talk! What sorrow awaits you who say to wooden idols, 'Wake up and save us!' To speechless stone images you say, 'Rise up and teach us!' Can an idol tell you what to do? They may be overlaid with gold and silver, but they are lifeless inside (NLT).

"They are lifeless inside." That's what you become when you worship something other than the sole source of life.

Isn't it interesting that what you fear, you worship, and what you worship determines who you will become? Wouldn't it be crazy if we had an enemy that wanted to be worshipped? I wonder how he would get us to worship him when we have such a worship-worthy God who provides such amazing benefits to worshipping Him?

This enemy would get you to listen to him, put faith in what he is saying, and then convince you with a few well-placed facts to fear him. We have an enemy who would love for you to fear him because then he can get you to worship him.

He is constantly on the prowl for this fear and worship. It's why Paul had to tell the Ephesians, "For you did not receive the spirit of bondage again to fear, but you received the Spirit of adoption by whom we cry out, 'Abba, Father'" (Romans 8:15).

The enemy constantly looks to trip us up in the fear of the wrong things (namely, him).

Satan even tried to get Jesus to worship him (Matthew 4:9). The enemy fell from heaven because he wanted to be like God (Isaiah 14:12-14), and he continues that pattern to this day. Satan wants you to fear him because he wants you to worship him.

Our enemy wants us to worship him to feed his own disgusting ego, but he also wants to rob the world of the image of God that you were created in—an image that only you can reflect to this world. As I've mentioned earlier, there is a part of who God is that He has placed inside of you that no one else can show this world. If the enemy can get you to fear him, worship him, and become bound, you will not be able to reflect who God is because you will not be engaging in the process of transformation into more

and more of who He created you to be! The stakes are
incredibly high.

———

There is a part of who God is that He has placed
inside of you that no one else can show this world

When God set His people free so that they could worship
Him, He was delivering them *from* Egypt, but He was also
desiring to deliver them *to* the Promised Land. Being
delivered *from* and being delivered *to* are two different
things entirely.

God set them free to worship in the desert, but we see that
they worshipped the wrong thing when they got there:

> Now when the people saw that Moses delayed coming down
> from the mountain, the people gathered together to Aaron, and
> said to him, "Come, make us gods that shall go before us; for as
> for this Moses, the man who brought us up out of the land of
> Egypt, we do not know what has become of him."

> And Aaron said to them, "Break off the golden earrings
> which are in the ears of your wives, your sons, and your
> daughters, and bring them to me." So all the people broke
> off the golden earrings which were in their ears, and
> brought them to Aaron. And he received the gold from their
> hand, and he fashioned it with an engraving tool, and made a
> molded calf.

> Then they said, "This is your god, O Israel, that brought you out
> of the land of Egypt!"

> So when Aaron saw it, he built an altar before it. And Aaron
> made a proclamation and said, "Tomorrow is a feast to the Lord."

Then they rose early on the next day, offered burnt offerings, and brought peace offerings; and the people sat down to eat and drink, and rose up to play (Exodus 32:1–5).

Can you imagine what that did to the heart of God? He did so many acts, so many efforts, so many signs, and so many plagues to bring His people to freedom to worship Him, and they worshipped something else.

I know that I've done this in my life. I've looked at all that God has done, and turned and worshipped the wrong thing. None of us are immune. When we are in the desert, in the quiet, we forget that we were brought there to worship Him, and we worship something else instead.

How could they, and how can we, even though we have been set free by God Almighty, worship the wrong thing even after He has done so much? The Israelites were brought out of Egypt, but Egypt still had to be brought out of them.

——

The Israelites were brought out of Egypt, but Egypt still had to be brought out of them.

Exodus 14 depicts the Egyptians being swallowed by the sea. It's an exciting victory for the Israelites in a battle that God fought for them. Wow did they worship God for that one! At the beginning of this story, we see something else though:

And when Pharaoh drew near, the children of Israel lifted their eyes, and behold, the Egyptians marched after them. So they were very afraid, and the children of Israel cried out to the Lord (Exodus 14:10).

The people were afraid of Pharaoh! You would hope that after a victory like this a switch would be flipped in their hearts, but time and again the people of Israel say, "We should have just stayed in Egypt where there was plenty of food. It would have been better there than to die here" (Exodus 14:12; 16:3).

The full expression of this is seen in Numbers 14:4. God has just shown them the land of Canaan—their Promised Land—and they say, "Let us select a leader and return to Egypt"! This is after miracle after miracle after miracle on their behalf. God showed them their Promised Land, and 10 out of 12 of the spies sent there to assess the situation said that they should tuck and run!

Clearly, they feared the wrong things (Pharaoh and Canaanites), and they worshipped the wrong things (golden calves and false gods). God had taken them out of Egypt, but He still needed to take Egypt out of them.

They had spent so long fearing the wrong things (and most likely worshipping the wrong things), that they needed to go into the wilderness for another 40 years to allow an entire generation to die.

When you look at the Promised Land and see a prison, you need freedom. When you look at the things and the people that God has for you, and fear overtakes you, you need freedom. You, like the Israelites, might just have been worshipping the wrong things. You might just need to get into His presence in a wilderness and have some things die.

———

When you look at the Promised Land
and see a prison, you need freedom.

God had to take the people of Israel through a process
of learning to fear Him. If you don't fear God, you will not
worship Him, because what you fear you worship, and
worship is the whole point of setting people free!

According to the U.S. Department of Health & Human
Services and a study by the University of California, Santa
Cruz, those who have spent time in prison leave with some of
prison still inside of them. Some call it a "prison mentality."
In this study, they list the following as characteristics of some
of those who are incarcerated: dependence on institutional
structure and contingencies, hypervigilance, interpersonal
distrust and suspicion, emotional over-control, alien-
ation, and psychological distancing, social withdrawal and
isolation, incorporation of exploitative norms of prison
culture, diminished sense of self-worth and personal value,
and finally, post-traumatic stress reactions to the pains of
imprisonment.[32]

We see some of these characteristics in the Israelites as
they venture through the wilderness, and if we were honest,
I think that we would acknowledge that each of us walks
through life with some if not many of these characteristics
ourselves. We have lived in bondage. We have been wrapped
in the chains of fearing all the wrong things. We need to
be free.

Someone today, reading this book, has been fearing the
enemy for so long that you have been worshipping him
and haven't even realized it. Like the people of Israel with

32. Haney, Craig. *U.S. Department of Health and Human Services.* 01
December 2001. November 2018. <https://aspe.hhs.gov/basic-report
/psychological-impact-incarceration-implications-post-prison
-adjustment>.

Pharaoh, you believe that he has more control and more influence over your future than God Himself. You have been a party to Satan getting his wish: to be elevated to the level of God. If he can do that in one life at a time, he is a few steps closer to his diabolical desire.

We must not fear the wrong things, no matter the cost.

"And I say to you, My friends, do not be afraid of those who kill the body, and after that have no more that they can do. But I will show you whom you should fear: Fear Him who, after He has killed, has power to cast into hell; yes, I say to you, fear Him!

"Are not five sparrows sold for two copper coins? And not one of them is forgotten before God. But the very hairs of your head are all numbered. Do not fear therefore; you are of more value than many sparrows" (Luke 12:4-6).

Fear God. He cares a whole lot about you.

Fear for Relationship

There's another reason that God would have us fear and worship Him: relationship.

God wants us to be close to Him! Worship is all about relationship.

Exodus 20:20–21 tells us,

And Moses said to the people, "Do not fear; for God has come to test you, and that His fear may be before you, so that you may not sin." So the people stood afar off, but Moses drew near the thick darkness where God was.

God wants you to fear Him and not to sin because sin is what separates us from Him. He wants to be close to us! Remember, the fear of the punishment of God separates us from Him. The fear of God draws us close.

> The fear of the punishment of God separates us from Him. The fear of God draws us close.

God loves you so much! He wants nothing more than to be close to you! Have you been feeling distant? Maybe you have been fearing the wrong things.

Finding Freedom from Fear

You cannot find freedom from fear by attempting to empty your life of fear. You will fear something. You were made to fear in the same way that you were made to worship. There is an altar on your heart. As we mentioned, something will always sit there because idols cannot be removed—they can only be replaced[33]

> You were made to fear in the same way that you were made to worship. There is an altar on your heart.

In the face of Pharaoh's threats, the midwives of the Israelite women refused to kill the newborn male babies.

---

33. Matt Papa, *Look and Live*. (Bloomington, MN: Baker Publishing Group, 2014.)

Why? Was it because they simply didn't fear Pharaoh? Scripture tells that it wasn't just because they weren't afraid of Pharaoh. It was because they feared God instead:

> But the midwives feared God, and did not do as the king of Egypt commanded them, but saved the male children alive (Exodus 1:17).

We often go through life trying not to be afraid of things. We try so hard to empty our lives of fear. We attempt to cast out the spirit of fear, but what do we invite to replace it?

If you recall, a swept but empty house is a very attractive place for evil spirits to return to.

> "When an unclean spirit goes out of a man, he goes through dry places, seeking rest, and finds none. Then he says, 'I will return to my house from which I came.' And when he comes, he finds it empty, swept, and put in order. Then he goes and takes with him seven other spirits more wicked than himself, and they enter and dwell there; and the last state of that man is worse than the first. So shall it also be with this wicked generation" (Matthew 12:43-45).

Have you ever fought the spirit of fear and thought you made some headway, but a short time later found yourself consumed by more fear than before? If you have, you have experienced this principle first hand. You cannot devoid your life of fear. You have to replace it.

The people of Israel were back to their homeland after a long captivity in Babylon. As good and exciting as this time was, they were surrounded by enemies. Imagine the fear that must have been present. Having just come out of captivity, and being surrounded by hostile or unknown countries, the fear of falling once again into captivity must have been enormous.

How did they respond?

> Though fear had come upon them because of the people of those countries, they set the altar on its bases; and they offered burnt offerings on it to the Lord, both the morning and evening burnt offerings (Ezra 3:3).

Though fear began creeping in, they chose to turn from their fears of man and to fear and worship God! This is what we must do in our lives. We must make a choice.

Though fear might be creeping in, though circumstances might look as big as a mountain, as threatening as Pharaoh, or as surrounding as hostile countries, we must choose to trade our fear of whatever it may be for a fear of God.

As we discovered earlier, you cannot fear two things at the same time. You have to make a choice.

> And of whom have you been afraid, or feared,
> That you have lied
> And not remembered Me,
> Nor taken it to your heart?
> Is it not because I have held My peace from of old
> That you do not fear Me? (Isaiah 57:11).

Here in Isaiah we see that God's people feared someone else, thus not fearing God. Again,

> "No one can serve two masters; for either he will hate the one and love the other, or else he will be loyal to the one

and despise the other. You cannot serve God and mammon"
(Matthew 6:24).

While this passage teaches us first and foremost that we
cannot serve God and mammon (the love of money), it also
re-presents us with the important principle that no one can
serve two masters. What you fear will master you; you cannot
fear God and something else at the same time. You must make
a choice.

———

What you fear will master you.

We must believe that God is above all else. We must believe
that He holds the ability to control our future. We must look
at everything in our lives through the filter of, "How does this
[thought, relationship, decision, etc.] affect the dynamic of
relationship between my God and me?"

It's not enough to understand fear. It's not enough to have
that knowledge in your mind, or even to know that you should
fear God above all else. You have to believe it.

What does belief look like? Belief is being fully convinced.
It's easy to believe that God is good, faithful, strong, our
provider, and more! Unfortunately, for many, it's only easy to
believe this for other people.

———

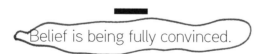

Belief is being fully convinced.

Are you fully convinced that who He is applies to you too?
Are you fully convinced that God is good?

Are you fully convinced that He is in control?

Are you fully convinced that He is all-powerful?

Are you fully convinced that He is who He says He is?

If you aren't, you will not fear Him, which means you will fear something else, and you will find yourself in bondage, becoming something that you never wanted to be.

The Fear Fight

I still have to fight off fear. Freedom from the fear you have isn't freedom from the fight. Jesus tells us that in this life we will have trials and tribulations, and often, these can feel like fights (John 16:33). Scripture also shares with us that we are in a battle,

> For we do not wrestle against flesh and blood, but against principalities, against powers, against the rulers of the darkness of this age, against spiritual hosts of wickedness in the heavenly places (Ephesians 6:12).

So what does fearing God do for us in this fight against fear?

First, fearing God gives you confidence. It gives you the confidence to know that all of the promises that come to those who fear God (many listed in Appendix B) are for you. No longer do you have to ask, "Do I fear God?" and wonder if you can lay hold of those promises that He makes. You can walk in confidence that you and your children will be protected, that you will have wisdom and knowledge and more!

Second, until you fear God, you will never be free. I realize this is a strong statement, but it is true. John 8:32 tells us, "And you shall know the truth, and the truth shall make you free." It's important to note from this verse that first comes knowing the truth, and then the truth is available to set you free.

———

Until you fear God, you will never be free.

The truth exists. God has written it in His Word. Freedom may be found. Freedom is a place, a state, a gift that God wants us to have. But, while truth exists and freedom may be found, you cannot find freedom until you receive the truth. The process of finding truth is called "knowing." Once you know the truth, then it will set you free. This "know" is the same "know" that John 10:14–15 uses when describing the relationship between Jesus and God and us and Jesus. It's an intimate knowing. We must *know* the truth.

Jesus sent the Holy Spirit to lead us into all truth (John 16:13), so we don't have to work, earn, fight, or push our way to truth. We just have to allow Him to lead us. Once there, though, we have to receive and *know*.

How do we know? On any journey or path, the first step is crucial. If you take the first step in the wrong direction, the next step had better be a course correction, or you will risk never arriving at your intended destination.

So what is the first step to knowledge? According to Proverbs 1:7, the fear of the Lord is the beginning of knowledge. If you don't fear the Lord, you will not take the first step to knowledge, which means you will not find knowledge, which means you will never know the truth, thus, never finding freedom.

If you don't fear the Lord, you will not find freedom. Do you fear the Lord? Great news: you are on your way to freedom! Freedom from what? Any bondage, including enslavement to fear of the wrong things!

Third, fearing God gives you authority. It gives you the authority to be able to respond rightly to the spirit of fear. When that lying prophetic spirit comes to you and tells you all of the things that you should be fearing, when he gives you the list of fears, all the reasons to fear them, and then coaches you on how to respond (shrinking back, turning off, holding back, staying quiet, etc.), you can stand up. You can stand up and say, "NO! I WILL NOT FEAR THAT! I FEAR GOD AND GOD ALONE, FOR HE IS THE ONLY ONE WORTHY OF MY FEAR!!!"

———

Fearing God gives you authority.

You now have the authority to stand where and how God called you to stand: victorious!

13

CONCLUSION

We are in a battle. There is no question of that. This truth does not vary from person to person or circumstance to circumstance. You are in a battle whether you recognize it or not.

The object of one's fear does vary from person to person and season by season. It's a choice each and every day of your life. The question is not if you will fight. You are reading this book because you are a fighter and fear has felt like the enemy. The real question is, *how* will you fight?

How will you fight?

Will you fight as you have always fought? Will you fight fear with the same tools and the same strategies? Will you continue to press and strive and work to live a life empty of fear? Will you work to arrange your world to avoid anything that may bring fear? This is impossible.

It might feel like the big, daunting, intimidating things of life make you fear, but someone else made you to fear. God made you to fear.

It's time to fight differently.

For you did not receive the spirit of bondage again to fear, but you received the Spirit of adoption by whom we cry out, "Abba, Father" (Romans 8:15).

Once you place your fear in God, there is no going back. You can allow God to take that place in your heart forever! I have had times in my life that were going well, and I was afraid that they might end. I lost out on of the joy of the season for fear that it might end. Maybe you are finishing this book thinking, *What if the fear of everything else comes back? What then?*

There are some things that never end. Just as Psalm 118 and Psalm 136 tell us that His mercy endures forever, so does the fear of Him:

> The fear of the Lord *is* clean, enduring forever;
> The judgments of the Lord *are* true *and* righteous
>   altogether (Psalm 19:9).

You can fear Him always! Even if you, like me, falter, waver, or fall, He is waiting with His arms open, ready to receive us again.

Cry out to Him. Fear Him. Worship Him.

Appendix A

STUDY GUIDE

Study Guide One

JOURNEY TOWARD FEAR

Key Thought

We must hear, have faith, and obey if we are going to overcome fear. Only then can we worship God and live truly free lives.

Key Scripture

John 10:10

"The thief does not come except to steal, and to kill, and destroy."

Discussion

- Why do you think fear affects every person, regardless of age, gender, or race?
- What does the enemy want to do to believers?
- Which of society's top fears do you relate to the most?

Activation

- Where do you think fear comes from? What purpose does it serve?
- Ask God, "What personal fears do I need to submit to You?"
- Think of a fearful situation from your past. Ask God to show you how He was with you during that time.

Study Guide Two

HEARING IS EVERYTHING

Key Thought

The messages we hear affect the way we see and interact with the world. Hearing is the reason we move from the comfortable known to the scary unknown where God is calling us.

Key Scriptures

Genesis 12:1–3

Now the Lord had said to Abram:
"Get out of your country,
From your family
And from your father's house,
To a land that I will show you.
I will make you a great nation;
I will bless you
And make your name great;
And you shall be a blessing.
I will bless those who bless you,
And I will curse him who curses you;
And in you all the families of the earth shall be blessed."

Discussion

- What is the first step on the path to fear?
- How does body language play a large role in nonverbal communication?
- What happens when nonverbal communication competes with verbal communication?

Activation

- Ask God, "What voices have influenced my life's direction until now?"
- Ask God, "Is there anything You've called me to do that I haven't done because it looks scary?"
- If there's anything you've stepped away from because of fear, repent for not obeying.

Study Guide Three

WHY HEARING IS EVERYTHING

Key Thought

God's voice will always agree with His Word and what it says about His nature and character. We must learn to hear God's voice in order to develop our relationship with Him and to have faith.

Key Scriptures

Isaiah 30:21

> Your ears shall hear a word behind you, saying,
> "This *is* the way, walk in it,"
> Whenever you turn to the right hand
> or whenever you turn to the left.

John 16:13

> "When He, the Spirit of truth, has come, He will guide you into all truth; for He will not speak on His own *authority*, but whatever He hears He will speak; and He will tell you things to come."

Romans 10:17

> So then faith *comes* by hearing, and hearing by the word of God.

Discussion

- What is the difference between a lie and the real truth?
- Why do you think Christians get caught up in "relation-ship with religion"?
- Describe a time when you were disappointed in God. Has hindsight changed your view of the situation?

Activation

- Practice listening for God's voice when you pray this week.
- Ask God to reveal any lies you believe about Him, your-self, or others.
- When praying for something specific, ask God, "Did I hear You, or is this just my own desire?"

Study Guide Four

FAITH

Key Thought

Faith comes by hearing. It keeps us moving forward in the face of opposition and carries us past fear. The only way we can please God is to put our faith in His Son, Jesus.

Key Scriptures

Hebrews 11:1

Now faith is the substance of things hoped for, the evidence of things not seen.

Hebrews 11:6

Without faith *it is* impossible to please *Him,* for he who comes to God must believe that He is, and *that* He is a rewarder of those who diligently seek Him.

John 16:33

"In the world you will have tribulation; but be of good cheer, I have overcome the world."

Discussion

- Why is it important for Christians to define faith properly?

- What is the difference between hope and faith?
- Why is hearing a requirement for pleasing God?

Activation

- Have you been listening to any human "logic" that might actually be the voice of the enemy?
- Ask God, "Have I been living from the wrong definition of faith?"
- Ask God to help you see His faithfulness, especially in times when you don't understand.

Study Guide Five

FEAR AND OBEDIENCE

Key Thought

You obey what you fear. If you aren't obeying God, you might be fearing something else. When we do obey God, we partner faith and works, and the result is justification.

Key Scriptures

Jeremiah 5:22–23

"Do you not fear Me?" says the Lord.

"Will you not tremble at My presence,

Who have placed the sand as the bound of the sea,

By a perpetual decree, that it cannot pass beyond it?

And though its waves toss to and fro,

Yet they cannot prevail;

Though they roar, yet they cannot pass over it.

But this people has a defiant and rebellious heart;

They have revolted and departed."

1 Samuel 12:14

"If you fear the Lord and serve Him and obey His voice, and do not rebel against the commandment of the Lord, then both you and the king who reigns over you will continue following the Lord your God."

Romans 10:9–10

If you confess with your mouth the Lord Jesus and believe in your heart that God has raised Him from the dead, you will be saved. For with the heart one believes unto righteousness, and with the mouth confession is made unto salvation.

Discussion

- Why does obedience follow fear?
- What are some common fears that we find ourselves obeying?
- Did you obey the last thing God asked you to do? Why or why not?

Activation

- Ask God, "Have I been giving attention to fear's voice or Your voice?"
- Ask God, "What do I fear most?"
- God asked Abraham to sacrifice Isaac. What has He asked you to sacrifice?

Study Guide Six

IS FEAR GOOD OR BAD?

Key Thought

By itself, fear is neutral; it only becomes good or bad when it is attached to positive or negative things. When we fear the wrong things, we become chained to them. When we fear God, we are free to go wherever He leads us.

Key Scriptures

Isaiah 8:12–13 (NASB)

"You are not to say, '*It is* a conspiracy!'
In regard to all that this people call a conspiracy,
And you are not to fear what they fear or be in dread of it.
It is the Lord of hosts whom you should regard as holy.
And He shall be your fear,
And He shall be your dread."

Luke 1:50

"And His mercy *is* on those who fear Him
From generation to generation."

Exodus 20:20 (NASB)

Moses said to the people, "Do not be afraid; for God has come in order to test you, and in order that the fear of Him may remain with you, so that you may not sin."

Psalm 112:1

Blessed *is* the man *who* fears the Lord,

Who delights greatly in His commandments.

Proverbs 14:2 (NLT)

Those who follow the right path fear the Lord;

those who take the wrong path despise him.

Discussion

- Which conclusion about fear have you believed in the past?
- What happens when fear is attached to the wrong thing?
- Why do you think God created fear?

Activation

- How has bad fear negatively impacted your life?
- Ask God, "To what (or whom) do I look for approval?"
- Ask God, "Do I fear You the right way?"

Study Guide Seven

IS FEAR ...?

Key Thought

Fear is an emotional response to danger and the root cause of stress. Fear itself is not a spirit, but there is a spirit of fear that wants us to shrink back from our God-given purpose.

Key Scriptures

2 Timothy 1:7–8

For God has not given us a spirit of fear, but of power and of love and of a sound mind. Therefore, do not be ashamed of the testimony of our Lord, nor of me His prisoner, but share with me in the sufferings for the gospel according to the power of God.

Numbers 13:32–33

And they gave the children of Israel a bad report of the land which they had spied out, saying, "The land through which we have gone as spies is a land that devours its inhabitants, and all the people whom we saw in it are men of great stature. There we saw the giants (the descendants of Anak came from the giants); and we were like grasshoppers in our own sight, and so we were in their sight."

Numbers 14:11

> Then the Lord said to Moses: "How long will these people reject Me? And how long will they not believe Me, with all the signs which I have performed among them?"

Discussion

- In what ways are fear and stress connected?
- How often does stress impact your life?
- How has the spirit of fear impacted someone you love?

Activation

- Think about the way fear plays a part of the stress in your life.
- Ask God, "Have I been listening to the spirit of fear or to You?"
- Ask God, "Have I been shrinking back from Your calling on my life?"

Study Guide Eight

THE POSTURE OF FEAR

Key Thought

The posture of fear is to fall down. When we get a glimpse of who God is, we fall in fear. Our fear is based not on what He can do but in who He is.

Key Scriptures

Isaiah 6:5 (NIV)

"Woe is me!... I am ruined! For I am a man of unclean lips, and I live among unclean people of unclean lips, and my eyes have seen the King, the Lord Almighty."

Ezekiel 1:26–28 (NIV)

High above on the throne was a figure like that of a man. I saw that from what appeared to be his waist up he looked like glowing metal, as if full of fire, and that from there down he looked like fire; and brilliant light surrounded him. Like the appearance of a rainbow in the clouds on a rainy day, so was the radiance around him.... When I saw it, I fell facedown."

Revelation 1:12–18 (NLT)

When I turned to see who was speaking to me, I saw seven gold lampstands. And standing in the middle of the lampstands was someone like the Son of Man. He was wearing a long robe with a gold sash across his chest. His head and his hair were white like wool, as white as snow. And his eyes were like flames of fire. His feet were like polished bronze refined in a furnace, and his voice thundered like mighty ocean waves. He held seven stars in his right hand, and a sharp two-edged sword came from his mouth. And his face was like the sun in all its brilliance. When I saw him, I fell at his feet as if I were dead. But he laid his right hand on me and said, "Don't be afraid! I am the First and the Last. I am the living one. I died, but look—I am alive forever and ever! And I hold the keys of death and the grave."

Discussion

- What is the goal of the spirit of fear?
- Why do you think the posture of fear begins in the heart and moves outward?
- Why does the posture of fear matter in regard to prayer?

Activation

- Ask God to reveal the posture of your heart.
- Ask God, "Do I tend to focus on my fear of the problem or on my fear of You?"
- Imagine you were Isaiah, Ezekiel, or John. What do you think your reaction would be if you came face-to-face with God?

Study Guide Nine

FEAR DEFINED

Key Thought

Fear is the heightened sense of awareness to the dynamic of relationship between two beings/things, which recognizes the severe superiority of one over the other, and its control of the outcome of one's future.

Key Scriptures

Hebrews 6:19

This *hope* we have as an anchor of the soul, both sure and steadfast, and which enters the *Presence* behind the veil.

Proverbs 14:2 (NLT)

Those who follow the right path fear the Lord;
those who take the wrong path despise him.

1 John 4:17–19

Love has been perfected among us in this: that we may have boldness in the day of judgment; because as He is, so are we in this world. There is no fear in love; but perfect love casts out fear, because fear involves torment. But he who fears has not been made perfect in love. We love Him because He first loved us.

Psalm 34:11

Come, you children, listen to me;
I will teach you the fear of the Lord.

Discussion

- How have you defined fear in the past?
- How is fearing God similar to fearing one's spouse?
- What is the difference between fearing God and fearing His punishment?

Activation

- In your own words, define fear.
- Ask God, "Have I made my relationship with You my top priority?"
- Ask God, "Have I allowed anything else to be number one in my life?"

Study Guide Ten

FIRST FEAR

Key Thought

When we fear God, it brings out the best in us. However, when we fear His punishment, we disappear and separate ourselves from Him.

Key Scriptures

Genesis 3:10 (NASB)

He said, "I heard the sound of You in the garden, and I was afraid because I was naked; so I hid myself."

Genesis 22:12 (NLT)

"Don't lay a hand on the boy!" the angel said. "Do not hurt him in any way, for now I know that you truly fear God. You have not withheld from me even your son, your only son."

Hebrews 11:17–19

By faith Abraham, when he was tested, offered up Isaac, and he who had received the promises offered up his only begotten son, of whom it was said, "In Isaac your seed shall be called," concluding that God was able to raise him up, even from the dead, from which he also received him in a figurative sense.

Discussion

- How does Dr. Henry Cloud define punishment?
- Why did Adam and Eve hide after they sinned?
- Does God want to punish you? Why or why not?

Activation

- Think about this statement: *Faith doesn't oppose fear; faith precedes it.*
- Ask God, "Do I fear You, or do I fear Your punishment?"
- Ask God, "Why did You punish Jesus on my behalf?"

Study Guide 11

WORSHIP

Key Thought

God created fear because fear leads to worship. When you fear the wrong thing, you worship the wrong thing.

Key Scriptures

Colossians 1:16

For by Him all things were created that are in heaven and that are on earth, visible and invisible, whether thrones or dominions or principalities or powers. All things were created through Him and for Him.

Ecclesiastes 3:14

I know that whatever God does,
It shall be forever.
Nothing can be added to it,
And nothing taken from it.
God does it, that men should fear before Him.

Deuteronomy 6:13 (NASB)

You shall fear only the Lord your God; and you shall worship and swear by His name.

1 Samuel 12:24(NASB)

"Only fear the Lord, and serve Him in truth with all your heart; for consider what great things He has done for you."

Discussion

- What is the difference between faith in God and the fear of God?
- What does Satan do to fear?
- What is the posture of fear?

Activation

- Ask God, "Have I worshipped things other than You?"
- Ask God, "How has fearing the wrong thing impacted my life?
- Think about this statement: *When you fear the wrong thing, you worship the wrong thing.*

Study Guide 12

FREEDOM

Key Thought

The fear of God draws us close to Him and sets us free. It gives us the confidence to know that all His promises are true, and it also gives us authority over the spirit of fear.

Key Scriptures

Romans 8:15

For you did not receive the spirit of bondage again to fear, but you received the Spirit of adoption by whom we cry out, "Abba, Father."

Luke 12:4–6

"And I say to you, My friends, do not be afraid of those who kill the body, and after that have no more that they can do. But I will show you whom you should fear: Fear Him who, after He has killed, has power to cast into hell; yes, I say to you, fear Him!

Are not five sparrows sold for two copper coins? And not one of them is forgotten before God. But the very hairs of your head are all numbered. Do not fear therefore; you are of more value than many sparrows."

Ephesians 6:12

> For we do not wrestle against flesh and blood, but against princi-
> palities, against powers, against the rulers of the darkness of this
> age, against spiritual *hosts* of wickedness in the heavenly *places.*

Discussion

- What is the definition of *bondage*?
- Why does God want us to fear and worship Him?
- Does God want us to be free? Why or why not?

Activation

- Think about this statement: Until you fear God, you will
  never be free.
- Ask God, "In what areas of my life do I need freedom?"
- Ask God to show you what He has done to set you free.

Appendix B

GOD'S PROMISES TO THOSE WHO FEAR HIM

Psalm 25:12

Who *is* the man that fears the Lord?
Him shall He teach in the way He chooses.

Psalm 25:14

The secret of the Lord *is* with those who fear Him,
And He will show them His covenant.

Psalm 25:14 (NLT)

The Lord is a friend to those who fear him.
He teaches them his covenant.

Psalm 33:18–19

Behold, the eye of the Lord *is* on those who fear Him,
On those who hope in His mercy,
To deliver their soul from death,
And to keep them alive in famine.

Psalm 34:7–9

The angel of the Lord encamps all around those who fear
     Him,
And delivers them.
Oh, taste and see that the Lord is good;
Blessed is the man who trusts in Him!
Oh, fear the Lord, you His saints!
There is no want to those who fear Him.

Psalm 60:4

You have given a banner to those who fear You,
That it may be displayed because of the truth.

Psalm 85:9

Surely His salvation *is* near to those who fear Him,
That glory may dwell in our land.

Psalm 103:11–12

For as the heavens are high above the earth,

So great is His mercy toward those who fear Him;

As far as the east is from the west,

So far has He removed our transgressions from us.

Psalm 111:5

He has given food to those who fear Him;

He will ever be mindful of His covenant.

Psalm 115:11

You who fear the Lord, trust in the Lord;

He *is* their help and their shield.

Psalm 128

Blessed is every one who fears the Lord,

Who walks in His ways.

When you eat the labor of your hands,

You shall be happy, and it shall be well with you.

Your wife shall be like a fruitful vine

In the very heart of your house,

Your children like olive plants

All around your table.

Behold, thus shall the man be blessed

Who fears the Lord.

The Lord bless you out of Zion,

And may you see the good of Jerusalem

All the days of your life.

Yes, may you see your children's children.

Peace be upon Israel!

Psalm 145:19

He will fulfill the desire of those who fear Him;

He also will hear their cry and save them.

Proverbs 14:26–27

In the fear of the Lord *there is* strong confidence,

And His children will have a place of refuge.

The fear of the Lord *is* a fountain of life,

To turn *one* away from the snares of death.

Proverbs 15:16

Better *is* a little with the fear of the Lord,

Than great treasure with trouble.

Proverbs 16:6

In mercy and truth

Atonement is provided for iniquity;

And by the fear of the LORD *one* departs from evil.

Proverbs 19:23

The fear of the LORD leads to life,

And he who has it will abide in satisfaction;

He will not be visited with evil

Proverbs 22:4

By humility *and* the fear of the Lord

Are riches and honor and life.

Proverbs 28:14 (NASB)

How blessed is the man who fears always,

But he who hardens his heart will fall into calamity.

Ecclesiastes 7:16–18

Do not be overly righteous,

Nor be overly wise:

Why should you destroy yourself?

Do not be overly wicked,

Nor be foolish:

Why should you die before your time?
It is good that you grasp this,
And also not remove your hand from the other;
For he who fears God will escape them all.

Ecclesiastes 8:12–13

Though a sinner does evil a hundred *times,* and his *days* are prolonged, yet I surely know that it will be well with those who fear God, who fear before Him. But it will not be well with the wicked; nor will he prolong *his* days, *which are* as a shadow, because he does not fear before God.

Isaiah 33:6

Wisdom and knowledge will be the stability of your times,
And the strength of salvation;
The fear of the Lord *is* His treasure.

Malachi 3:16

Then those who feared the Lord spoke to one another,
And the Lord listened and heard *them;*
So a book of remembrance was written before Him
For those who fear the Lord
And who meditate on His name.

Malachi 4:2

But to you who fear My name
The Sun of Righteousness shall arise
With healing in His wings;
And you shall go out
And grow fat like stall-fed calves.

Luke 1:50

And His mercy *is* on those who fear Him
From generation to generation.

Revelation 11:18

"The nations were angry, and Your wrath has come,
And the time of the dead, that they should be judged,
And that You should reward Your servants the prophets and the saints,
And those who fear Your name, small and great,
And should destroy those who destroy the earth."

Appendix C

GOD'S COMMANDS TO FEAR NOT

Genesis 21:17

And God heard the voice of the lad. Then the angel of God called to Hagar out of heaven, and said to her, "What ails you, Hagar? Fear not, for God has heard the voice of the lad where he *is.*"

Genesis 26:24

And the Lord appeared to him the same night and said, "I *am* the God of your father Abraham; do not fear, for I *am* with you. I will bless you and multiply your descendants for My servant Abraham's sake."

Genesis 35:17

Now it came to pass, when she was in hard labor, that the midwife said to her, "Do not fear; you will have this son also."

Genesis 46:3

So He said, "I *am* God, the God of your father; do not fear to go down to Egypt, for I will make of you a great nation there."

Exodus 20:20

And Moses said to the people, "Do not fear; for God has come to test you, and that His fear may be before you, so that you may not sin."

Numbers 14:9

Only do not rebel against the Lord, nor fear the people of the land, for they *are* our bread; their protection has departed from them, and the Lord *is* with us. Do not fear them."

Numbers 21:34

Then the Lord said to Moses, "Do not fear him, for I have delivered him into your hand, with all his people and his land; and you shall do to him as you did to Sihon king of the Amorites, who dwelt at Heshbon."

Deuteronomy 1:21

Look, the Lord your God has set the land before you; go up *and* possess *it,* as the Lord God of your fathers has spoken to you; do not fear or be discouraged.

Deuteronomy 3:2

And the Lord said to me, "Do not fear him, for I have delivered him and all his people and his land into your hand; you shall do to him as you did to Sihon king of the Amorites, who dwelt at Heshbon."

Deuteronomy 31:6

"Be strong and of good courage, do not fear nor be afraid of them; for the Lord your God, He *is* the One who goes with you. He will not leave you nor forsake you."

Deuteronomy 31:8

And the Lord, He *is* the One who goes before you. He will be with you, He will not leave you nor forsake you; do not fear nor be dismayed.

Joshua 10:8

And the Lord said to Joshua, "Do not fear them, for I have delivered them into your hand; not a man of them shall stand before you."

Judges 6:10

"Also I said to you, 'I *am* the Lord your God; do not fear the gods of the Amorites, in whose land you dwell.' But you have not obeyed My voice."

Judges 6:23

Then the Lord said to him, "Peace *be* with you; do not fear, you shall not die."

Ruth 3:11

And now, my daughter, do not fear. I will do for you all that you request, for all the people of my town know that you *are* a virtuous woman.

1 Samuel 12:20

Then Samuel said to the people, "Do not fear. You have done all this wickedness; yet do not turn aside from following the Lord, but serve the Lord with all your heart."

1 Samuel 22:23

Stay with me; do not fear. For he who seeks my life seeks your life, but with me you *shall be* safe."

1 Samuel 23:17

And he said to him, "Do not fear, for the hand of Saul my father shall not find you. You shall be king over Israel, and I shall be next to you. Even my father Saul knows that."

2 Samuel 9:7

So David said to him, "Do not fear, for I will surely show you kindness for Jonathan your father's sake, and will restore to you all the land of Saul your grandfather; and you shall eat bread at my table continually."

1 Kings 17:13

And Elijah said to her, "Do not fear; go *and* do as you have said, but make me a small cake from it first, and bring *it* to me; and afterward make *some* for yourself and your son."

2 Kings 6:16

So he answered, "Do not fear, for those who *are* with us *are* more than those who *are* with them."

1 Chronicles 22:13

Then you will prosper, if you take care to fulfill the statutes and judgments with which the Lord charged Moses concerning Israel. Be strong and of good courage; do not fear nor be dismayed.

1 Chronicles 28:20

And David said to his son Solomon, "Be strong and of good courage, and do *it;* do not fear nor be dismayed, for the Lord God—my God—*will be* with you. He will not leave you nor forsake you, until you have finished all the work for the service of the house of the Lord.

Isaiah 41:10

Fear not, for I *am* with you;
Be not dismayed, for I *am* your God.

I will strengthen you,

Yes, I will help you,

I will uphold you with My righteous right hand.'

Isaiah 41:13

"For I, the Lord your God, will hold your right hand,

Saying to you, 'Fear not, I will help you.'"

Isaiah 41:14

"Fear not, you worm Jacob,

You men of Israel!

I will help you," says the Lord

And your Redeemer, the Holy One of Israel.

Isaiah 43:1

But now, thus says the Lord, who created you, O Jacob,

And He who formed you, O Israel:

"Fear not, for I have redeemed you;

I have called *you* by your name;

You *are* Mine."

Isaiah 43:5

Fear not, for I *am* with you;

I will bring your descendants from the east,

And gather you from the west;

Isaiah 44:2

Thus says the Lord who made you

And formed you from the womb, *who* will help you:

"Fear not, O Jacob My servant;

And you, Jeshurun, whom I have chosen."

Daniel 10:19

And he said, "O man greatly beloved, fear not! Peace *be* to you; be strong, yes, be strong!"

So when he spoke to me I was strengthened, and said, "Let my lord speak, for you have strengthened me."

Joel 2:21

Fear not, O land; Be glad and rejoice, For the Lord has done marvelous things!

John 12:15

"Fear not, daughter of Zion; Behold, your King is coming, Sitting on a donkey's colt."

ABOUT THE AUTHOR

BENJAMIN GILMORE is an Equip pastor at Gateway Church, where he has attended since 2005 and worked since 2012. He has served the church in areas of worship and prayer as well as freedom, where he managed KAIROS (Gateway's flagship Freedom event) and taught Freedom classes. In his current role, Benjamin continues to lead Freedom classes, and he also develops curriculum, oversees Southlake Equip teachers, and participates in the integration of freedom culture throughout the church.

Benjamin holds a bachelor's degree in mathematics and a master's degree in Business Administration with focuses on leadership, entrepreneurship, and innovation. He also has several years of international sports ministry. Together, his education and experiences give Benjamin a unique perspective of God's Word for our lives today.

The greatest joys of Benjamin's life are his wife and daughter.